VULTURE CITY

VULTURE CITY

CITY

HOW OUR BANKERS GOT
RICH ON SWINDLES

TOM RAVLIC

'Tom Ravlic lays it all out with forensic precision in *Vulture City: How Our Bankers Got Rich on Swindles*.

Backed with an implied government guarantee, Australia's banks have been exposed drooling over their customers as a source of unearned or gouged income. Just how did this culture develop? Where were the regulators who are meant to protect consumers, particularly those who most needed protection… from themselves?

Tom takes us right to the destruction of trust that should be at the very foundation of a country's banking and financial systems. And he charts a course for future regulatory and corporate rigour as a first step to restoring that trust.'

QUENTIN DEMPSTER, FORMER HOST, 7.30 REPORT, ABC

'Tom Ravlic has written a hard-headed and hard hitting – yet highly readable – account of the events leading up to the Hayne Royal Commission.'

PROFESSOR SINCLAIR DAVIDSON, PROFESSOR OF INSTITUTIONAL ECONOMICS, RMIT

'Tom Ravlic points the finger squarely at greed as the driving force in this thorough investigation of banking misbehaviour. Read it and, literally, weep.'

KERRY-ANNE WALSH, AWARD WINNING AUTHOR
AND POLITICAL JOURNALIST

'Tom's journalism is based on old fashioned forensic research.'

STEPHEN CONROY, FORMER ALP SENATOR AND
SKY NEWS COMMENTATOR

'This book gives a remarkable insight into one of the darkest chapters in Australia's financial sector. Tom Ravlic has shone a light on a system that was not only broken but needed fixing. He has cleverly and judiciously honed in on the key drivers that contributed to a collapse in confidence in the banking sector. This book is compulsory reading for those wanting to understand what happened.'

PETER GLEESON, SKY NEWS ANCHOR AND
NEWS LIMITED COLUMNIST

Published by:
Wilkinson Publishing Pty Ltd
ACN 006 042 173
Level 4, 2 Collins Street
Melbourne, Vic 3000
Ph: 03 9654 5446
www.wilkinsonpublishing.com.au

NATIONAL LIBRARY OF AUSTRALIA

A catalogue record for this book is available from the National Library of Australia

Planned date of publication: 10-2019
Title: Vulture City
ISBN(s): 978-1-925927-02-3: Printed - Paperback

Design by Alicia Freile, Tango Media
Printed and bound in Australia by Ligare Pty Ltd

Dedication

This book is dedicated to my parents, Katica and Jozip Ravlic,
and my brother Rob, sister-in-law Sally and my two effervescent,
energetic nephews, Mason and Archer, without whom
life would be a grey, drab existence.

CONTENTS

||||||||||||||||||||||||||||||||||||||||||||

FOREWORD

IIIIIIIIIIIIIIIIIIIIIIIIIIIIIIIIIIIIIIIIIIII

In the mid-1990s, the Commonwealth Bank launched its financial services business. The media launch became something of a publicity debacle because the journalists honed immediately on the clear conflict of interest of banks selling financial products. The explanation, at the time, was telling and inadequate: 'We will always sell the best products to our customers,' is how I remember it. But of course, that can never be true... no financial product can ever, always, be the best. The other telling news of that day was how tellers would be financially encouraged to pass on customer leads to financial planners who, in turn, were paid commissions. Welcome to the new world of banking. It was the start of a slow-moving car crash that eventually sparked a royal commission, though 20 years too late for many of the victims of ethically compromised banks. Tom Ravlic dissects the evolution of those conflicts in this book, through his forensic re-telling of the events leading up to and inside the royal commission. As I reflect on the past 30 years in financial services, a key tangential point – to me – seems to be the rush to demutualise, corporatise and then stock market list previous mutual style businesses. Think here about some of the heavily criticised players of the royal commission: the 173-year-old IOOF (listed in 2003), the 170-year-old AMP (listed in 1998) and even the formerly Federal Government owned Commonwealth Bank, created in 1911 and listed in 1991. The cultural move from being for-members, or customers, to being for-profit was clearly a step too far for these organisations to deal with. Hence the criticism from the royal commission – as told by Ravlic – that profit and the shareholders' interest outweighed those of the customers (who, in mutual organisations, are also the effective owners). Modern financial services executives, I think, could do well to visit a statue in central Sydney, just a block away from AMP's headquarters. That statue is of Thomas Sutcliffe Mort, who arrived in Australia in 1837 and 12 years later helped found the Australian Mutual Provident Society. It says he was '...foremost in every movement for the care and welfare of his fellow citizens, who in gratitude erected this monument to his memory.' Think on those words: 'the care and welfare of his fellow citizens'. I suspect no such monument will be erected for the bank or insurance executives who presided over these giant institutions in the decade or so before this royal commission, who in many cases did not care for the welfare of their fellow citizens.

Ross Greenwood
Finance Editor, Channel Nine

INTRODUCTION

||||||||||||||||||||||||||||||||||||||||||||

*'I thought nothing could shock me anymore, but in
my forty years as a journo, most of it covering business,
I have never seen anything as appalling as what we
are witnessing at the banking RC. And I covered
the '80s crooks including Bond and Skase.'*

JANINE PERRETT, SKY NEWS PRESENTER AND BUSINESS JOURNALIST

'Avarice, the spur of industry.'

DAVID HUME

THE ROYAL COMMISSION into Misconduct in the Banking, Superannuation and Financial Services Industry, also known as the Hayne Royal Commission, was primarily focused on the behaviour of banks, brokers and other professionals that have, through their vulture-like conduct, caused serious financial pain to clients and, more broadly, the community. It was a royal commission that was sought after by concerned politicians and journalists who had identified some years before that there were issues in the banking sector that needed the scalpel-like inquisition from well-trained, probing legal minds to expose the absence of ethics, empathy, risk management, quality controls, international best practice board and committee practices, and quality control in the corporate culture of financial institutions that seems to ape in every possible way the scene from the Michael Douglas blockbuster *Wall Street*. 'Greed – for lack of a better word – is good,' Douglas' character, stock broker Gordon Gecko, opined. 'Greed works, greed is right. Greed clarifies, cuts through, and captures the essence of the evolutionary spirit.' Those words in part epitomised the 1980s – the decade in which the stock market took a dive of 22% on the Dow Jones. To assume that underlying ethos characterised in those words should apply only to the decade that brought Australia's first America's Cup win; Michael Jackson's *Thriller*; Tom Cruise in *Top Gun*; the Reagan presidency; the start of a lengthy term in office for the Australian Labor Party; and corporate miscreants Alan Bond and Christopher Skase is to misunderstand the human condition and what ultimately drives some people when they are invited by their employer, through use of financial incentives, to prioritise their bank account over the fundamental duty of care that an adviser ought to exercise in the provision of financial advice to clients.

Greed was placed centre stage under a searing spotlight as a key cause of most of the issues that Commissioner Hayne, a former High Court judge with a no-nonsense demeanour, encountered as he and the Commission's legal team pored over the submissions to choose case studies that best represented the broad range of problems the Commission was trying to better understand in order to propose a remedy. Much of the evidence heard by Commissioner Hayne and his team of crack legal minds gradually put together the mosaic that gave them a picture: the financial services sector was rife with misbehaviour and breaches of the law. According to the interim report's executive summary, Commissioner Hayne noted greed was one of the factors that played a role in a situation characterised by a diminished level of trust in the financial services sector. 'Banks, and all financial services entities, recognised that they sold services and products. Selling became their focus of attention. Too often it became the sole focus of attention. Products and services multiplied. Banks searched for their "share of the customer's wallet",' said Hayne. 'From the executive suite to the front line, staff were measured and rewarded by reference to profit and sales.' The perspectives of some people in the banking sector were skewed towards the generation of revenue at the expense of the customers' welfare. This phenomenon was all too common and occurred in almost every case that came before the commissioner and his team. Some of the worst examples are highlighted in all their inglorious detail in the pages that follow.

Commissioner Hayne expressed reservations in his interim report about the fact that misconduct of various kinds may have been uncovered but nothing of real consequence was done by the regulatory bodies such as ASIC and APRA to either punish the perpetrators of the conduct nor create a deterrent for others wishing to pilfer the hard earned savings of clients. 'The conduct regulator, ASIC, rarely went to court to seek public denunciation of and punishment for misconduct. The prudential regulator, APRA, never went to court,' Commissioner Hayne noted. 'Much more often than not, when misconduct was revealed, little happened beyond apology from the entity, a drawn out remediation program and protracted negotiation with ASIC of a media release, an infringement notice, or an enforceable undertaking that acknowledged no more than that ASIC had reasonable "concerns" about the entity's conduct.' Financial penalties handed to banks were hardly material and there were also negotiated amounts that constituted community benefit payments as part of enforceable undertakings, which is an agreement between the regulator and an individual or entity, that were also a drop in the bucket of the revenues the banks raked in over any given year.

Commissioner Hayne is not the only judicial voice that has pointed to issues with the regulators responsible for the financial services sector. Justice Neville Owen noted during his careful autopsy conducted on the corpse of HIH Insurance, for which the final report was released in 2003, that ASIC revealed a degree of impotence in that circumstance, preferring to leave much of the heavy regulatory lifting to the prudential regulator, APRA. While Justice Owen was critical of APRA and its conduct, the final report of the commission was scathing of the corporate regulator. 'ASIC limited its involvement on HIH's affairs because of a perception that APRA was responsible for and was in fact closely and effectively monitoring the situation,' Justice Owen said. 'ASIC considered it had little direct responsibility in relation to prudential regulation of insurers.' Justice Owen noted his disagreement with ASIC's interpretation of the split between ASIC and APRA in terms of their supervisory or regulatory role over HIH. Commissioner Hayne's two reports pointed to enforcement weaknesses and recommended greater, more focused power for both ASIC and APRA. Only time will tell what effect a renewed focus on enforcement and court action will have on the governance culture of entities. At the time of writing it was clear that ASIC had begun the process of tightening the thumbscrews with surveillance and also a greater willingness to use powers of public hearings to hold financial institutions to account. These are encouraging developments but monitoring and scrutiny by the Federal Parliament, consumer groups, the media and other stakeholders is necessary to ensure the regulator delivers.

PROFESSIONAL BODIES AND THEIR PROCESSES

Extra-legal processes that are undertaken by professional bodies or associations for dealing with breaches of professional standards came under fire during the royal commission because they were observed to not have sufficient power to properly deal with bad behaviour beyond the most extreme punishment being expulsion. Bodies such as the Financial Planning Association and the Association of Finance Advisers were subjected to examination at the hearings in order to explore the nature of professional discipline with Commissioner Hayne expressing concern about the length of time it took to deal with issues. The final report recommended a fundamental change in the statutory disciplinary regime, with the report setting out a thumbnail sketch of a new disciplinary regime for financial advisers that will have details added, presumably once government has consulted or, more poignantly, negotiated with the targets of this regulation.

Hayne's prescription would have all financial advisers registered as individuals and that registration, their ticket to a river of money if they do it ethically, can be yanked from them if they engage in unlawful conduct.

The prescription put forward by the Commission is hardly novel. Tax agents, auditors and liquidators operate in a similar fashion. A model based on Hayne's recommendation would result in an individual financial adviser being dealt with because it would be their behaviour that had caused grief to a client or clients. This creates an incentive for a person providing advice to behave in an ethical manner because they would be unable to hide behind organisational management, an incentive scheme or key performance criteria set down in the performance plans. The company does not lose registration – the adviser does. It becomes a question of what is right for the client, rather than what is the 'right advice' to line one's pockets as an adviser within a corporate culture that might have made a virtue of enriching oneself by meeting key performance indicators driven by sales.

Employers of financial advisers would be obliged to report their own team members when breaches became apparent for a disciplinary reckoning but other parties, consumers and professional bodies and regulators amongst others, would be able to report them as well. It is entirely possible that an adviser that is rotten to the core could be reported twice to the statutory disciplinary board but equally plausible is the prospect that only one party reports misconduct. This recommendation is aimed at cleaning up poor practice when it surfaces because individual registration and punishment means advisory firms cannot bury sins of recalcitrant, noncompliant and penny-pinching advisers for too long.

What Commissioner Hayne and his team of inquisitors were confronted with was a financial services sector that had through its own pursuit of profits thrown caution to the wind. The bastions of prudence had become home to individuals that were being rewarded for amoral, rapacious and self-interested behaviour. There were cases where the conduct of staff corrupted even the processes of self-regulation that existed within organisations to the point where internal controls were useless. A hunger for personal financial gains led over time to the fraying of the ethical fabric within financial institutions, with the only significant winners being spivs and their bosses wanting to drain blood from a stone for one more dollar of commission, for which they never managed to grow a dislike. Revelations from whistle blowers and others point to specific advisers, bankers, insurers and others being treated as if they were a protected species, provided they were rainmakers. Commissioner Hayne's reflection on greed explains what we have observed only in part but his assessment in that executive summary is simply a contemporary articulation of an issue that has centuries of precedent in the studies of and writings on the behaviour of people in positions of trust.

The question that must be asked is how the lessons from this exercise in the dredging up of causes of human misery and financial distress stay in the public conscience. In my personal experience the details of reviews, royal commissions and inquiries fade undeservingly into obscurity as people go back to their daily lives free from the saturation coverage of acts of fraud, deception and poor disclosure or explanation of significant personal transactions being carved up in a court room. This book is intended to highlight some of the misconduct to raise consumer awareness and encourage people to go into discussions with any institution – not just banks – armed with a heightened sense of scepticism and a preparedness to ask critical questions to protect their own financial or other interests.

WHO CAN PEOPLE TRUST?

||||||||||||||||||||||||||||||||||||||||||||||||

'Australians engage financial advisors to improve their financial position, to achieve their aspirations, and to plan for their future. Clients repose trust and confidence in their financial advisors. It is important that their trust and confidence is well placed.'

ROWENA ORR QC, COUNSEL ASSISTING

'Every new fiduciary relation is an opportunity for a breach of trust.'

EDWARD ALSWORTH ROSS

AUSTRALIANS HAVE been faced with uncomfortable truths about various institutions in which individuals or groups of individuals ought to be able to place unconditional trust. The country has made a habit of establishing one inquiry after another to peer into darkness. Each of these inquiries has revealed examples of exploitation, negligence and self-gratification at the expense of victims that were often not spared much thought or offered remediation until long after the events that caused them emotional, physical or financial distress had occurred. A royal commission, held from 2013 to 2017, into institutional responses to child sexual abuse opened the floodgates to painful memories for many people betrayed by individuals in responsible positions that even parents trusted would keep their children safe. Child protection and youth detention systems in the Northern Territory were examined following media coverage from 2016 to 2017. Royal commissions into the safety and quality of aged care and violence, abuse, neglect and exploitation of people with disabilities were either in progress or set to commence at the time of writing. Each of these royal commissions tackled to a greater or lesser extent a central question: can people that have our most vulnerable people in their care be trusted to do so without greater regulatory intervention? The brutal reality in each case is that the trust so many individuals or their families had in the systems that are supposedly set up to help and not hinder their progress in life was betrayed. In the case of the financial services sector this betrayal was accompanied by monetary incentives paid to the agents of financial institutions that were apparently fulfilling the objectives set down under key performance indicators.

The trust deficit in financial institutions, which is the focus of this book, and the dissatisfaction consumers had with the behaviour of these corporate behemoths was and remains a central theme in the public discourse concerning the behaviour of banks in their quest for redemption. It should, however, not be something that surprises anybody given that examples of exploitation and theft of the vulnerable, the weak and the financially illiterate will remain etched in the minds of those that observed the royal commission. The behaviours the royal commission highlighted, and Commissioner Hayne sought to remedy in his recommendations, are in no way new. People have been stealing, in one form or another, from each other since time began. The means by which crimes against property are committed might have become more sophisticated with the advent of technology but human nature has not advanced much at all.

Consider the observations made in various texts from different periods of history – religious texts or otherwise – about human nature and what those sources say about acts we would define as being different kinds of criminal conduct today. A prominent example of this are the 10 commandments in the Old Testament of the Bible with its simple, erudite 'Thou shalt not steal'. Modern versions of those commandments modernise the English phrasing to 'You shall not steal', but the point remains the same. The commandments also include other matters that would later be covered in criminal codes, such as murder. What the commandments provide is a code of conduct of some description that lays down expectations of behaviour.

It is important in the context of financial services, however, to consider how theft morphs in an environment where fiduciary duties of a slightly more modern kind come into play. This was brilliantly articulated by sociologist Edward Alsworth Ross. Ross was the author of a book published in 1907 called *Sin and Society: An Analysis of Latter Day Iniquity* and in it he writes on the manner in which the notion of sin in society changes as society itself develops and morphs. He reflects specifically on what we would later come to know as white collar crime by observing that some of the old sins are being upstaged by methods being used by a new class of sinner. 'Gamester, murderer, body-snatcher and kidnapper may appeal to a Hogarth, but what challenge finds his pencil in the countenance of the boodler, the savings-bank wrecker, or the ballot-box stuffer,' Ross said. 'The modern high-power dealer of woe wears immaculate linen, carries a silk hat and a lighted cigar, sins with a calm countenance and a serene soul, league or months from the evil he causes.' Ross described these unsavoury characters that move in high societal circles as 'criminaloids' that occupy 'cabins rather than the steerage of society'.

'Relentless pursuit hems in the criminals, narrows their range of success, denies them influence,' Ross observed. 'The criminaloids on the other hand encounter but feeble opposition, and, since their practices are often more lucrative than authentic crimes, they distance their more scrupulous rivals in business and politics and reap an uncommon worldly prosperity.'

It should also be borne in mind that Ross considered the criminaloid guilty of moral insensibility rather than pure evil. 'Nature has not foredoomed them to evil by a double dose of lust, cruelty, malice, greed, or jealousy. They are not degenerates tormented by monstrous cravings,' said Ross. 'They want nothing more than we all want – money, power, consideration – in a word, success; but they are in a hurry and they are not particular as to the means.' The latter observation is a perfect description of what the Commissioner and counsel assisting encountered over the year during which they grilled executives, senior managers and advisers about the way in which they deal with client issues but with an important twist: there was always one or more laws, regulations, ethical principles or community standards and expectations being trampled on by certain individuals in order to get their hands on dough.

The modern 'sinner' in Ross' day was some rungs above the brawling street thieves and pick pockets on the ladder of activity but the substance of corporate sin, if you will, and white collar crime is the same irrespective of the advances in technology and the development of different methods of financing that appear to emerge from the dark arts of financial alchemy to ordinary folk. It is difficult to find fault with Ross' logic when one reflects on the way in which shares might have been traded in the early part of the 20th century with paper-based certificates while in the age of the information superhighway that has simply gotten faster and bigger, the criminal can steal identities, launder funds through multiple bank accounts and con good hearted citizens into donating via a website for what they think is a charity but is a front for funding terror activity. Anti-money laundering regulation is of global significance and one of Australia's largest financial institutions, the Commonwealth Bank, fell foul of laws designed to ensure that money being transferred through banks by crooks or terror merchants is tracked. There were multiple cases of what were said to be breaches of responsible lending rules in the law across a range of institutions. Some of those were linked to people getting incentive-based payments for convincing a customer they needed a financial product that would handcuff them to debt while the adviser's bank account had a cash transfusion. Those groups or individuals that wish to do others harm for their own enrichment and other purposes will find ways of using modern methods of transacting business to achieve their goals.

Ross' thoughts about sin and society and corporate charlatans he called 'criminaloids' predate the work done by Edwin Sutherland and other thinkers on white collar crime. Sutherland defined crime by looking at the offender that in his view would be the top echelon in any corporate environment, being senior managers, chief executive officers and business managers. It is problematic, however, to just consider the offender in this context. What happens to the definition of a white collar criminal if a person who is a chief executive officer happens to steal a wallet? Does that make the chief executive officer's theft of a wallet a white collar crime merely because he or she holds that position within an entity? Different perspectives developed that shifted from focusing on a specific offending demographic, such as senior management in companies, to examining offences more closely.

Advances in thinking about what some refer to rather mistakenly as victimless crime is the framework proposed by Herbert Edelhertz. Edelhertz's work was cited in the 1978 Congressional report into the federal response to the problem of white collar crime and his definition focused on an illegal act or series of illegal acts committed by nonphysical means and by concealment or guile, to obtain money or property, to avoid the payment or loss of money or property or to obtain business or personal advantage. The contrast between the focus placed on the offender in the first instance when the term was coined to the focus on the nature of offences committed cannot be starker. It must be acknowledged at this point that not everything touched by the royal commission and discussed here is related to breaches of civil or criminal law. It would be folly for anyone to suggest otherwise. Consider the circumstances of a bank engaging a liquidator to sell a property and force a farmer and family to vacate a property without looking at other opportunities to keep the famer on the land and re-establish a facility. Commission Hayne reflected on the banks' use of corporate power throughout and – while a bank may be entitled to send debt collectors in their various forms after customers in default – their frequent use of corporate power without compassion. Most people can tell right from wrong, but what Commissioner Hayne was pointing to was the necessity of achieving an outcome that was not just right from the point of view of black letter law but an outcome that was more just, compassionate and, indeed, merciful in the circumstances.

CORPORATE CULTURE

There is a question that is asked by people whenever they are confronted by acts that are horrid, unexpected or unconscionable. It is the most common and simplest question in the world: why? Why have the largest companies in the country, that purportedly look after the finances of many tens of thousands of individuals, turned into entities that appear to be organisations in which financial advisers and other employees have commissions fed into them by intravenous drip? How did the culture of the Commonwealth Bank's financial planning arm in New South Wales, for example, turn south during the late 2000s and become one where fleecing customers became a sign of success and not one of complete and depraved moral collapse? These situations always have some element of pursuit of self-interest about them but this does not offer an explanation of why the entire system was compromised during that period.

The Commonwealth Bank whistle blower, Jeff Morris, explained the cultural decay within the financial planning arm in evidence to a Senate committee hearing into the effectiveness of ASIC, Australia's corporate regulator. The culture within the financial planning arm of the bank was driven by the rewards system. Some people within the bank sought to use the incentive-based payments structure of banks to their own advantage with some of the behaviour exhibited by advisers, tellers, brokers and bankers fitting precisely within the definition of what criminologists call 'the fraud triangle'. The three factors considered in the 'fraud triangle' are the existence of pressure or incentive to commit fraud, the opportunity within the workplace to commit a fraudulent act and also the ability to rationalise the acts in some form. It is clear from evidence outlined by Morris in his materials and in case studies aired during the Hayne exercise that the incentives and opportunities were there in abundance for those wishing to misbehave to do so. Opportunities that may not have existed had proper internal audit and quality review processes been conscientiously maintained and the findings appropriately acted on by those same financial institutions now paying tens of millions in remediation payments to customers exploited by their agents, branch managers or other staff. Much of this behaviour that resulted in customers' accounts being bled dry at the CBA and elsewhere was occurring while political leaders were praising the robustness of our banks during the worst of the global financial crisis. It is an open question as to whether this assessment of Australia dodging the bullet during the global financial crisis ought to be tempered by further reflection on the behaviour of those individuals driven by an objective of self-enrichment that was enabled by incentives set for them by their masters in the company they served.

This was not the only case of corporate conspiracy against vulnerable 'prey' that had turned to experts for advice but were ultimately let down, betrayed and left seeking compensation. Consider the examples of forging of signatures, opening of accounts in the name of children without parental authorisation to get kickbacks; charging dead people for services they had no way of 'using'; charging living people for services that were never delivered; granting of credit to gambling addicted customers; deliberate overriding internal para-planning advice in order to get commissions; setting receivers onto farmers who were to the point of despair when loan books looked sour; industrial scale document fraud in situations where companies needed to hide evidence of inappropriate advice; and lies told to a corporate regulator about the state of compliance with financial services laws. This is scratching the surface of the things bankers and advisers have done in the name of self-interest, scoring a profit to please shareholders and to make the bank look like a worthwhile investment for those managing portfolios for institutional investors and superannuation funds.

In the case of AMP and its executives, they failed to play the honest broker with the corporate regulator, the Australian Securities and Investments Commission, multiple times. Evidence tendered to the royal commission could lead to the conclusion AMP misled the commission and the harsh public light that was shone on these events eventually led to the resignation of Catherine Brenner, the former chair of the AMP board in the midst of the public relations backlash following the revelations of dishonesty and inappropriate behaviour in the delivery of financial advice.

A media release issued by AMP on 30 April 2018 announced Brenner's departure from the top job and offered the following observations from Brenner herself. 'I am honoured to have been Chairman of AMP. I am deeply disappointed by the issues at hand and am particularly concerned for the impact they have had on our customers, employees, advisers and shareholders. As Chairman, I am accountable for governance. I have always sought to act in the best interests of the company and have been in discussions with the Board about the most appropriate course of action, including my resignation.'

AMP was not the only entity that wound up with changes to those that are both in charge of and set the tone for governance. Commonwealth Bank's chief executive Ian Narev was replaced by Matt Comyn, with the bank making more personnel changes over time. Comyn famously cited Narev as having told him to 'temper his sense of justice' during discussions on withdrawing a product that Comyn felt was not beneficial for customers. NAB chairman Ken Henry and Andrew Thorburn, the bank's chief executive officer, both resigned their posts following scathing commentary from Commissioner Hayne about their commitment to a change in the culture at the bank.

POINTING FINGERS

There is a need, however, to address the phenomenon of the mob baying for blood following misconduct by financial services entities. Sanctions against boards of directors, senior management and staff have been discussed in the media and elsewhere, which is understandable given the impact of the misconduct in both human and financial terms. It is necessary to contemplate with some care the responsibilities of boards of directors, senior management, leaders of business lines and the middle managers involved in these organisations. Some degree of fact finding is necessary before blame is laid at the feet of a board for the activities of a rogue planner or their immediate supervisor. It is unrealistic to expect that a board of directors would know that there is a rogue planner or teller or adviser somewhere in their system. It is impossible for a board member to know that one person or several people in a branch in one corner of a country has created their own fiefdom of greed or corruption within the business. Directors should be able to trust the system that is overseen by the management they employ to work prudently and ethically as a general principle. The role of directors should never be confused with that of management and it is foolish to expect that the activities of a rogue staffer seeking to line their own pockets will be known by the board.

Populist calls for the heads of chairmen and directors of boards to be thrown behind bars may be an understandable reaction to one or many transgressions committed by a corporation, but it is hard, cold evidence and not emotion that must drive judicial outcomes. It is the fact patterns that will ultimately determine the parties that are guilty of offences where matters are tried before a court of law. There will, of course, be times when a director or an entire board will find themselves in a public prosecutor's cross-hairs for what has occurred within an entity over which they have oversight. Only a fool would suggest otherwise. One thing is certain, however, and that is that shareholders end up paying dearly for unethical conduct engaged in by those working within and managing the entity in which they have an ownership stake.

REVISITING NEVILLE OWEN

The issues raised above only scratch the surface when it comes to addressing the issues of corporate morality in the context of Australia's financial services sector. It is both enlightening and depressing to read the words of Justice Owen reflecting on corporate morality and corporate awareness of misconduct in the context of the HIH collapse in light of the more recent royal commission into the broader financial services sector. 'From time to time as I listened to the evidence about specific transactions or decisions, I found myself asking rhetorically: did anyone stand back and ask themselves the simple question – is this right?' Justice Owen said in a two-page personal perspective on his experience in chairing the HIH Royal Commission. The royal commissioner noted that there was a growth each year in the volume of law with which companies need to comply and, while these rules were necessary for the orderly functioning of society, it 'would be a shame if the prescription of corporate governance models and standards of conduct for corporate officers became the beginning, middle and the end of the decision making process'. Justice Owen's 'ideal world' would result in people commencing a decision-making process by asking whether the actions being proposed are 'right'. 'That would be the first question, rather than: how far can the prescriptive dictates be stretched?' Justice Owen noted. 'The end of the process must, of course, be in accord with the prescriptive dictates, but it will have been informed by a consideration of whether it is morally right.'

Concepts of right and wrong and what actions may be good or bad do not exist – as Justice Owen noted – outside of a context. 'I think all those who participate in the direction and management of public companies, as well as their professional advisers, need to identity and examine what they regard as the basic moral underpinning of their system of values. They must then apply those tenets in the decision-making process.'

One can add to Justice Owen's pithy observations of the need for corporations to have a moral compass the repeated refrain throughout the interim and final reports of the Hayne Royal Commission of conduct that did not meet community expectations or community standards. That grounds the discussion in what is fair and just in a moral sense and not merely on what can pass muster under the interpretation of statute or common law.

It should be noted that many of the case studies of activities documented during the year-long deep dive into aspects of the financial sector generally featured large organisations that have values and mission statements that are easily identified. Any company of any size could point to an annual report, internal code of conduct, a risk management manual, notes or minutes of meetings, pages emblazoned with 'About Us' on a website or lodgements with various regulators as evidence of values. These published values are nothing more than cladding on a decaying timber frame if the values remain unenforced by the tacit – even unspoken – approval of misconduct within a corporate structure. Australia's banks and financial institutions have all got multiple publications in which their corporate vision and asserted values are written but these mean nothing if in various parts of an organisation there are termites eating away at the structure. Shareholders, customers, ratings agencies, market analysts and the media need evidence and assurance that the banks and other institutions have the necessary internal controls and policing in place to reflect what they say are their cultural values.

Any changing of regulation or process requires courage and a determination of a hierarchy within governments themselves, government departments, statutory boards, regulators such as ASIC and APRA, listed corporations, financial planning firms and the many professional associations that have members that play some part in the provision of advice to non-expert consumers that they hope is in their best interests. It became apparent during the process of writing this book that implementation of the Hayne Royal Commission's recommendations would inevitably become a yardstick by which politicians measured the seriousness of the need to fix those ills that populated the transcripts of the hearings. The keeping of score in these circumstances is not necessarily an altogether altruistic endeavour and neither major political party in Australia is completely immune from criticism. Any reluctance to action recommendations, such as the curbing of commissions for transactions facilitated by mortgage brokers, for example, would be and was seen by cynical commentators as a sign of administrative weakness and a tip of the hat to political self-interest in the lead up to the Federal Election ultimately won by the Morrison-led Coalition.

It is to be expected that the Hayne list of recommendations will continue to be used as a 'device' to measure how seriously political parties value the work of the royal commission, but that approach is of limited value in the longer term. The interim and final reports of the Hayne Royal Commission will gather dust like the reports of all the royal commissions preceding it and parliamentary committee hearings related to banks, accounting firms and audit practices will be held to drill deeper into other parts of corporate Australia left unmined by Commissioner Hayne due to limitations of scope. Consistent and persistent reviews of the inner workings of professional firms, banks and other organisations are necessary to ensure that the lessons from Hayne remain in the public consciousness. Regulators such as APRA, ASIC and, indeed, professional associations must also be prepared to make life uncomfortable for those regulated by them as tension between the regulator and the regulated is necessary for a healthy fear to exist between the two and for the required culture of compliance to exist. A more profound question, however, to which there is no easy answer is how companies within the financial services sector can ensure they create an environment over the long term where they achieve financial success and provide services of benefit to clients while also ensuring they discourage – through their own vigilance and diligence – the kind of conduct revealed during the royal commission that can emanate from the darkest parts of human hearts.

CONSUMER ATTITUDES TOWARDS BANKS

One survey by accounting firm Deloitte serves to illustrate the attitude towards the financial services sector and banks in particular. Deloitte surveyed 2,072 people in 2018 and found the general attitude of people towards banks was poor. The survey results showed:

- Only 21% believed that banks generally had customer interests at heart,
- 26% believed banks would keep their promises,
- 20% saw banks as being generally ethical and doing what is good, right and fair, and,
- 32% believed that regulators were doing enough to hold banks to account.

This is only one survey and but it provides a sense of the feeling that existed in the marketplace during the royal commission. It should be said, however, that the same group of respondents gave more positive answers when it came to their individual experiences with their own bank. Consider the following responses that mirror the first two questions mentioned above; 36% of those responding to the survey thought that their bank had their best interests at heart, and 49% felt their bank would keep its promises. It should be noted that neither of these results had a majority of respondents giving the banks plaudits.

TURNBULL:
A CONSCRIPT TO A CAUSE

||||||||||||||||||||||||||||||||||||||||||||||||

'Victory has a thousand fathers, but defeat is an orphan.'
JOHN F. KENNEDY

'So I think while we regret the necessity of the decision that we've taken, it is in the national economic interest.'
MALCOLM TURNBULL, PRIME MINISTER

'Anyone robbing with a pen needs to get looked at.'
JOHN 'WACKA' WILLIAMS, NATIONAL PARTY SENATOR

TRYING TO ATTRIBUTE the final calling of a royal commission to any single source is an exercise in futility. Any person sifting through the voluminous pile of material related to the behaviour of the banking sector for the best part of a decade will see influences that would have their own contribution to make in the discussion and debate leading to the Hayne inquisition. It depends on the sources consulted by an interested punter as well as their ability to cut through what politicians and some media pundits would call the 'nuance' of political debate. There are a range of protagonists from different sides of the political fence, whistle blowers, consumer groups, investigative journalists and bank customers that played a role over the better part of a decade to bring about an awareness of an unforgiving performance driven, rapacious and amoral culture within the financial services sector that they argued required the intervention of the most powerful mechanism of inquiry available in Australia. A royal commission is no small undertaking and the human and other resources such an inquisitorial intervention requires come at considerable cost with the Hayne Royal Commission clocking in at around $70 million.

What is certain, however, is that the coalition government is unlikely to have called a royal commission but for two factors that created the tipping point: the rebelliousness of National Party members and senators, and a special pleading from the chairs and senior management of four major banks in separate initiatives. It should be noted that a royal commission into the Don Dale in the Northern Territory was announced the following morning by Turnbull after a *Four Corners* report aired on the ABC but no similar reaction was seen from the Abbott-led administration when *Four Corners* aired a report in May 2014 fronted by Adele Ferguson into the Commonwealth Bank and the way in which it focused more on selling to rather than empathising with and caring for customers.

The Coalition Government's assertion that it can claim credit for the calling of a royal commission can at best be described as disingenuous and is reliant on the crutch of incumbency for its legitimacy. The resistance the coalition demonstrated over an extended period of time to the calling of a royal commission allowed other actors to continue their agitation for a royal commission. This prolonged activism, which was in part facilitated by the multiple parliamentary committees inquiring into the financial services sector, ensured the government was eventually forced to call a royal commission on its terms rather than have a parliamentary commission of inquiry with terms drafted by Senators and Members of Parliament that could have a broader remit. The tipping point was clearly reached when both the banking sector and the Liberal Party's coalition partner used different tactics to pressure the prime minister – a reluctant conscript to a royal commission's cause – to cave in. A tipping point had been reached and the banking sector itself had written correspondence designed to provide the government with a trigger for the calling of a royal commission into the financial services sector so that a terms of reference can be crafted outside of the influence of parliamentary forces that may wish to extend its reach beyond what the Hayne Royal Commission was ultimately asked to consider. Any responsible analysis of factors that led to the calling of the royal commission requires – indeed demands – a survey of the broader landscape before dealing with the final point at which the Turnbull Government surrendered to a pincer movement that neither Turnbull nor his then treasurer, Scott Morrison, were able to resist. The role of other actors and institutions is just as – if not more – important in ensuring a royal commission materialised because it was their contribution and persistence that led to this end. Any objective analysis of the situation would also conclude that the problems highlighted by the Hayne inquiry had already appeared in a range of other committees' examinations of financial services regulation. The ultimate contribution by Hayne would be the creation of a cumulative ugly mosaic of individual and institutional misconduct across all areas of banking, financial advice, superannuation, insurance and, indeed, the corporate governance of some of Australia's largest corporations.

SOME PREVIOUS FINANCIAL PLANNING SCANDALS

Financial collapses and rip-offs of investors are nothing new in Australia and prior to the global financial crisis unfolding Australian investors were severely burned. The financial well being was affected by poor advice that led them to invest in products linked to a series of investment companies that had operations that dive bombed. The Financial System Inquiry chaired by former Commonwealth Bank Chief Executive Officer David Murray issued a final report that outlined estimated total losses of more than $5 billion, or $4 billion after compensation and recoveries by liquidators. These were not insignificant losses for businesses that were hell bent on flogging product at the expense of a customer's financial security. The final report of the Murray Review, which took place in 2014, said that the collapses of finance businesses including Storm Financial, Opes Prime, Westpoint, Great Southern, Timbercorp and Banksia Securities affected more than 80,000 people.

In the case of Storm Financial the company flogged advice that was based on getting clients into debt to buy shares. The clients would take out loans secured against their properties and invest in shares of ASX 300 companies. Many clients found themselves in financial distress as a result of this advice. Storm Financial losses totalled more than $3 billion with 3,000 of the company's 14,000 clients being in an adverse position after implementing the advice that Storm Financial gurus had given them. The collapse of Storm was the subject of a parliamentary inquiry in 2009. The chairman of that committee, Bernie Ripoll, said that 'Although the committee cannot make judgements about unlawful conduct, there were clearly multiple failures by Storm Financial and some lending institutions. By recommending aggressive leveraged lending strategies to elderly people on low incomes, Storm's advisers were not providing advice that was appropriate to their clients' needs. Both Storm Financial and the margin lenders who provided credit to their clients, particularly the Commonwealth Bank, mishandled issuing margin calls when the market was in decline.'

There was a finding that would later become just as significant during another more powerful inquiry a decade later: banks were lax in the way they lent money to clients that were in no position to repay the loans when the investment at which they threw the borrowed funds tanked.

Ripoll also pointed to the system of remuneration operating in the financial services sector at the time of the committee's report to parliament in 2009. Remuneration structures led to consumers getting advice that was aligned to the best interests of the adviser rather than the interests of the client seeking to grow their portfolio.

'We have also recommended that the government consult with the industry on the best way to cease payments from product manufacturers to financial advisers, such as commissions and volume bonuses,' Ripoll noted in a media release issued at the launch of the report from the committee. 'The conflicts of interest created by these payments are not always managed properly and should be removed to improve trust and confidence in the industry.'

Owners of the Storm Financial business, Emmanuel and Julie Cassimatis, ended up in court some years after the collapse of the company. They were found to have breached duties of care and diligence under the Corporations Act because the way they ran the business caused poor or inappropriate advice to be given to people. In March 2018 the couple were each hit with fines of $70,000 and a seven-year ban from managing corporations when the Federal Court found they were focusing more on making a buck rather than paying attention to their vulnerable clients. Not all of Storm's clients were impressed with the Federal Court's decision with one former client, Vietnam veteran Stephen Reynolds, telling ABC News on 23 March 2018 that he was saddled with $1.2 million debt and lost his house as a result of dealing with Storm Financial. He told the ABC that the fines made no sense to him because people lost their life savings and their lives had been destroyed.

Stockbroking firm Opes Prime, which fizzled into non-existence and left a trail of destruction behind it, was also the subject of the Ripoll committee's scrutiny. It had a business model that was different to Storm Financial but similar criticisms existed regarding the impact of the advice provided by the company and the fact there were terms in the contracts related to the equity finance deals Opes Prime was offering that were at best opaque. Opes was involved in securities lending, which is similar to a margin loan. A client was given cash by Opes Prime using their shares as security for the loan. The title to the shares, however, transferred to Opes Prime rather than be mortgaged. ASIC told the Ripoll committee that this method was not commonly used by retail investors. Banks that held securities as collateral for finance given to Opes Prime sold the securities when the stock broking firm was put into administration. Retail investors were unable to do anything in relation to the shares they had transferred to Opes Prime because they no longer had the title. They could not get back to their original financial position.

Submissions received by the Ripoll committee outlined problems with understanding the contractual terms. 'I am an investor who has suffered significant financial loss as a result of the collapse of Opes. I am not a greedy person attracted by the promise of high returns,' said one respondent to the committee who requested anonymity. '[Rather] I am an educated, financially literate person (at the time I entered into the Opes agreement I was working as a Licensed Adviser), who was misled and deceived by Opes personnel as to the true nature of their "margin lending" product.' Another submission from Robert Fowler had pointed to the fact that his shares – and that of other investors – were used by Opes to enter into arrangements with ANZ. He told the committee that this element of the transactions was not communicated at the time. 'The news filtered out that this was an absolute transfer of title to the bank and that our only claim was against Opes Prime stockbroking. My world had effectively ceased to exist,' Fowler said.

The committee found that the Opes Prime arrangements were unsuitable for retail investors and that the level and clarity of disclosure of the arrangements left much to be desired. There was an anonymous submission that suggested clients of Opes Prime should have been asked to sign a risk disclosure statement. 'If a client had been required to sign a simple risk disclosure statement stating, for instance, that the client acknowledged that they had lost beneficial ownership of and legal title to their shares; and furthermore that their shares were being used as collateral by Opes for financing purposes – many people would not have signed,' the anonymous respondent said.

These case studies from 2008 and 2009 – at the height of the global financial crisis – had elements that would again emerge as being contentious when other committees and inquiries kicked the tyres of the financial services sector some more. The Hayne inquiry would also revisit these issues in a more public, forensic and – at least for the institutions subject to grilling – near-humiliating fashion.

OPENING UP THE FRONT FOR MORE PROBES

The first revelations of industrial scale misconduct in certain divisions of the big four banks, particularly the Commonwealth Bank, began to appear more broadly during 2013. The publication of stories in June 2013 that were written for the then Fairfax papers *The Age* and the *Sydney Morning Herald* by Adele Ferguson contained key revelations of the corruption of internal controls within the Commonwealth Bank that led to particular planners making good coin at someone else's expense. These stories and other media accounts of bank misconduct and the absence of appropriate remediation payments to clients prompted politicians and other stakeholders to begin asking further questions about the manner in which the banks were behaving. It was from that point that Senators in the Australian parliament began to reflect on how best to bring about some kind of intense, more forensic examination into the behaviour of banks and the regulatory system that was supposed to be protecting the consumer. While the role of the media was significant in raising awareness, it was the pressure placed on the Turnbull administration by political forces that would eventually lead to the calling of the Hayne Royal Commission.

PERFORMANCE OF ASIC – SENATE ECONOMICS COMMITTEE (2014)

Members of the Senate Economics Committee heard evidence of misconduct by banks and it received evidence from victims of misconduct, former staff from the banking sector, bank executives and ASIC. It was the first parliamentary exposition of the circumstances that were publicly exposed by whistle blowers from within the Commonwealth Bank. ASIC and the bank came under fire for their failure to deal appropriately with those engaging in misconduct. Clients of the CBA expressed their concerns about the bank's behaviour towards them and highlighted conduct they believe deserved greater consequences under the law. Allegations of misconduct included the preparation of inappropriate advice for clients, the forgery of signatures on documents without client consent, document fraud designed to retrofit financial advice and the payment of bribes by financial advisers so that colleagues would refer work directly to them rather than process it as required through the system. It should be borne in mind that some members of the committee had been observing trends in the misconduct engaged in by financial institutions since the Storm Financial and Opes Prime collapses were probed. Certain behaviours would hardly have been a surprise.

The committee recommended a range of measures that related to boosting financial literacy, encouraging consumers to get independent advice and also for the corporate regulator to improve its monitoring of breaches. Recommendation seven of the committee report suggested the government hold a royal commission or judicial inquiry that would:

■ Thoroughly examine the actions of the Commonwealth Bank of Australia (CBA) in relation to the misconduct of advisers and planners within the CBA's financial planning businesses and the allegations of a cover up.

■ Identify any conduct that may amount to a breach of any law or professional standard.

■ Review all files of clients affected or likely to be affected by the misconduct and assess the appropriateness of the compensation processes and amounts of compensation offered and provided by the CBA to these clients; and,

■ Make recommendations about ASIC and any regulatory or legislative reforms that may be required.

'This is not a recommendation that the committee has made lightly, but the evidence the committee has received is so shocking and the credibility of both ASIC and the CBA is so compromised that a royal commission really is warranted,' said Bishop, the committee chair at the time. 'The CBA's focus is on downplaying the extent of wrongdoing and minimising the amount of compensation it has to pay. Meanwhile, ASIC has shown that it is not sufficiently sceptical of the CBA's actions and cannot hold it to account.'

Bishop said that the Commonwealth Bank financial planning scandal that was at the centre of this particular committee hearing should be treated as a lesson by the broader financial services sector and that 'firms need to know that they cannot turn a blind eye to rogue employees who do whatever it takes to make profits at the expense of vulnerable investors'.

The Federal Government, led by then prime minister Tony Abbott, refused to entertain the notion of a royal commission into the banking sector. 'There have been several Senate Committee and other inquiries into these and related issues in recent years, including the very comprehensive inquiry by this Committee,' the government response said. 'Since the Committee has reported, the Senate has also initiated a further inquiry related to these same issues. Instead of initiating another inquiry, in relation to CBA Financial Planning, the Government considers that the most important focus must be on resolving any legitimate outstanding grievances from affected customers.' The government was also keen at that time to see the results of the Open Advice Review Program established by the Commonwealth Bank, which involved an Independent Review headed by Ian Callinan, for former High Court Justice.

This committee inquiry hit a hurdle during the preparation of its report for the parliament because there was new information about the inconsistent manner in which the compensation for Commonwealth bank clients was being handled. The committee chair at the time, Senator Mark Bishop, said in a media release that both ASIC and the CBA had contacted the committee because further issues with the compensation scheme were identified. 'Although ASIC and the CBA have attempted to correct the record, the committee found that the evidence provided was sketchy and has left many key questions unanswered,' the media release said. 'Critical information is lacking on how many affected clients were kept in the dark by the CFP, and for how long, and the number who missed out on the offer of $5,000 to help them pay for an expert assessor to assist their claim.'

This report was also released during a period when a partisan tussle was breaking out in the Senate over changes to the Future of Financial Advice reforms that were, according to critics of proposed changes to the legislation, watering down client protections such as the level of disclosure required by advisers to clients. Parliamentary debates descended into name calling with Labor Senator Doug Cameron suggesting the long-time crusader against the financial services misconduct, John Williams, had gone from being Batman of DC Comics fame to the Joker because he spoke in favour of changes to the FOFA legislation in debate. The Labor Party was amongst those that believed the amendments to rules for more frequent fee disclosures to clients would lower the level of consumer protection.

GREENS MOTION IN THE SENATE ON 24 JUNE 2015

Australian Greens Senator Peter Whish-Wilson moved a motion calling for a royal commission into misconduct into the banking sector, which was defeated on the floor of the Senate by both the Coalition and the Australian Labor Party. Senator John Williams was the sole voice from the coalition to cross the floor and call for a royal commission into the sector. 'It is time for a broad-ranging royal commission in this country into white collar crime and misconduct in the financial services sector,' Whish-Wilson said. 'Nearly 12 months ago, the Senate inquiry of the Economics Committee made a recommendation for a royal commission into the Commonwealth Bank. Following that, in the last 12 months, thanks to some brave whistle blowers and some dogged reporting from Fairfax journalists, we have seen allegations and revelations of misconduct at Macquarie Bank, ANZ, National Australia Bank and, recently, at IOOF. How many more scandals are lurking under the surface?' Whish-Wilson acknowledged the work of parliamentary committees but that was insufficient.

The Federal Government was unmoved and Senator Mitch Fifield said that the government's position had not changed since they responded to recommendations in the final report from the inquiry into the performance of the corporate regulator. 'The financial services industry has never been under closer scrutiny. Over the past 12 months alone we have had five inquiries into the sector,' Fifield said. 'The Financial System Inquiry made recommendations to strengthen regulation of the financial advice sector and increase ASIC powers, as did the Economics Committee inquiry into the performance of ASIC.'

SENATE INQUIRY INTO THE SUPERVISION OF FINANCIAL ADVICE

A further inquiry was started into financial services by the Senate Economics Committee soon after kicking the tyres of the regulator and finding the corporate cop wanting. This inquiry looked at a range of methods in which financial advice was provided and it heard more evidence of misconduct. One of the major focuses for this committee was something the committee referred to as land banking. Evidence examined by the committee showed that there were highly speculative schemes in which investors had placed funds at the urging of property spruikers. The committee chairman at the time, Senator Chris Ketter, said that there was an absence of clarity about whether people were able to identify good advisers from bad when it comes to property investment. The committee found a litany of problems with the manner in which property investments were marketed to unsuspecting retail investors with risks of investments downplayed in promotional materials. There were also concerns about commissions related to the flogging of investments in property that were considerable and created an incentive for the property spruikers to sell the investments to as many people as they possibly could. 'It is very concerning that many Australians may not be aware that their speculative property investments could be a tragedy in the making,' Ketter said. 'Let's be clear on this, not all property investments are shonky, but it is unclear whether ordinary Australians can tell the difference between a low risk and high risk investment, particularly when the property spruiker has given them highly professional materials implying that a proposed development is already in the planning phase when the reality may be that it is a piece of bush with no planning approval.' Investors were expecting estates with a range of features from modern architecture, recreational space and helipads. The committee found that there were parts of the land promoted for these purposes that remained in a relatively undeveloped state.

The committee also published a 50-page discussion paper on whistle blowers, their importance and various measures that can be undertaken to ensure that whistle blowers are given some benefit for their assistance in reporting misconduct. It should be noted at this point that the parliamentary committee called former Commonwealth Bank financial planner and whistle blower, Jeff Morris, to give further evidence at this committee.

TWO MOTIONS, TWO PARTIES – ONE OBJECTIVE

The Labor Party and the Greens moved separate motions referring to the calling of a royal commission into the financial services sector on 16 April 2016 in the Senate. The motions referred to the need to have an all-powerful body to call the financial services entities before it to determine the causes of misconduct. Senator Scott Ryan responded in a similar fashion to both motions for a royal commission. 'The government recognises that Australia's banks and banking executives have not always lived up to the standards expected by the community, but the government does not support appointing a royal commission into banking and financial services,' Ryan said on behalf of the Coalition government. 'The government continues to support our regulators in ensuring the integrity of our finance and banking system, ensuring consumer protections are watertight and ensuring that malpractice is punished. A royal commissioner has no power to enforce the law, whether through taking prosecution action against a person or body, making findings of a breach of law, or imposing fines or penalties.' Enhanced Labor interest in a royal commission was also due to the proactivity of then senator Sam Dastyari, who could sense the need for an inquiry but also political gains to be made given the government's steadfast refusal to bend.

FURTHER SENATE MOTION CALLING FOR A ROYAL COMMISSION – 1 SEPTEMBER 2016

Labor Senator Penny Wong moved a motion in the Senate calling for the establishment of a royal commission into the banking sector. That motion, which was passed by the Senate, was opposed by the Federal Government with Senator James McGrath stating that the government believed there was no benefit to consumers or the economy at large. 'Whilst the government has proactively sought to reform Australia's financial sector, Labor when in government sat idle and oversaw scandal after scandal. In fact, most of the notable scandals and collapses happened on Labor's watch, when the Leader of the Opposition was the Minister for Financial Services and Superannuation, including financial planning scandals at the Commonwealth Bank and Macquarie and the collapse of firms such as Trio Capital, Storm Financial and Great Southern,' McGrath said. 'Labor was in government for six years and did not act. Our government has acted. We have delivered the Financial System Inquiry and a stronger regulator with more resources and powers, and we are working on a one-stop shop for consumer complaints.'

Labor Senator Katy Gallagher said that there were people who had come to hear the motion debated and passed in the public gallery of the Senate who had shared their experiences with the banking sector. She said she had spent an hour with the people who had reports of bank misconduct on the day the motion was due to be put.

'Listen to the stories of those people whose lives have been affected, whose houses have been lost, whose retirement savings have vanished, whose businesses have folded and who have been arguing for years – eight to 10 years, for some people – for some sense of justice. This is what this motion seeks and that is what a royal commission will find,' Gallagher said.

Senator John Williams disputed the wording of the motion during discussion on the floor because he wanted an amendment to it to specifically refer to life insurance, but Senator Peter Whish-Wilson said that the concerns Williams had were already addressed by the wording of the motion. 'I want to point out to the chamber and espe-cially to you, Senator Williams – I first, of course, recognise that you have called for a royal commission into financial misconduct for some time, and I respect that – that the banks are now vertically integrated,' Whish-Wilson stated. 'If we have an inquiry into the banking system, that includes the insurance markets. Most banks own financial services companies, including insurance companies. So the motion put by Labor I support, because it will encompass the areas of your concern.'

ANOTHER SENATE MOTION CALLING FOR A PROBE – 1 DECEMBER 2016

There was a second motion passed in 2016 calling for a royal com-mission. It was moved by Labor's Gallagher in the Senate on behalf of the Labor Party and Senator Rod Culleton on 1 December 2016. Culleton was elected as a part of the unprecedented four Senate seat jackpot that Senator Pauline Hanson scored as a part of the double dissolution. Culleton had dealt with bankers in his private affairs as well as sharing the concerns about bank misconduct held by other farmers in Western Australia and elsewhere. Culleton had drafted a terms of reference and it was tabled by him as a part of the motion to pressure the government into calling a royal commission. There was no government response to this motion but the National's Williams made another call for the royal commission to be broad. 'We should broaden it to take in all white collar crime. We should broaden it to take in industry super funds and the fees that they have siphoned off to the unions and then into Labor's war chest,' Williams argued. 'I wonder if people in this chamber are aware that, as I read recently, over the past two years industry super funds paid more than $5.4 million to unions and the ACTU, with a fair portion of that flowing to the Labor Party.'

Williams was the only Senator to make any contribution of substance on this occasion.

CULLETON OUT OF THE SENATE

Culleton was booted from the Senate as a result of an unresolved bankruptcy. He was unable to continue his crusade for a royal commission because between 1 December 2016 when he tabled a motion calling for a royal commission and early January 2017, the then Senator Stephen Parry had declared his term to be over as a result of a breach of Section 44. Culleton's period as a Senator in the Australian parliament was characterised by conflicts with One Nation leader Pauline Hanson. Footage of Hanson asserting her leadership via a television news camera to get Culleton to attend her office received enormous publicity. It was also noted in media reports that there were disputes or altercations between the Hanson office and Culleton's staff – evidence that not everything was particularly smooth in the parliamentary wing of the minor party. *The Guardian* reported on 6 December 2016 that Hanson stated Culleton would not listen to reason and therefore she and her other colleagues could not work with him. An illustration of the acrimony between the two at that point in time was the split between Culleton and Hanson on the backpacker tax and the split between the two Senators on initiating a banking royal commission. Hanson and Culleton did not see eye to eye on issues related to the rate at which the backpacker tax should be pegged. The Western Australian Senator's proposal for a banking royal commission was also not something that received his then party leader's support despite the One Nation leader's support for a banking royal commission during the 2016 election. He was replaced in the Senate by his brother-in-law, Peter Georgiou: the second cab off the rank on a three-person ticket that was a family affair. Culleton's wife, Ioanna, was third on the ticket. Culleton maintained an active interest in the banks after leaving parliament and promoted private prosecutions as a way of getting remediations for bank misconduct.

BANKING AND FINANCIAL SERVICES COMMISSION OF INQUIRY BILL 2017

The first attempt at getting a parliamentary commission of inquiry established was coordinated by the Australian Greens in the Senate but was accompanied by the names of a slew of cross-bench Senators. Senators Whish-Wilson, Hanson, former broadcaster Derryn Hinch, Jacqui Lambie, Malcolm Roberts and Nick Xenophon sponsored the Bill that was first introduced on 22 March 2017. 'As the custodians and intermediators of other people's money, the banking and finance sector are granted a privileged position in our society,' Whish-Wilson told the Senate in the second reading speech. 'This privilege is evident in the guarantees provided by government regarding the continued operation of the sector. This includes explicit government guarantees on deposits and liquidity, and an implicit government guarantee backing those institutions that are too-big-to-fail.' Whish-Wilson further told the Senate that trust in financial institutions had broken down and needed to be restored. The Bill passed the Senate on 15 June 2017. While it was introduced in the House of Representatives, it fizzled in the lower house due to lack of support.

SELECT COMMITTEE ON LENDING TO PRIMARY PRODUCTION CUSTOMERS

The agricultural sector has been one of the hardest hit by banking misconduct and the Select Committee looking at primary production customers of banks sought evidence from famers about the manner in which they were treated by banks. This inquiry was chaired by One Nation Senators. Roberts assumed the chairmanship from the inception of the inquiry but he was later replaced by Hanson when the High Court ruled him ineligible given he had not renounced his citizenship of the United Kingdom in time for the 2016 Federal Election. It was an inquiry that sought to get evidence about the treatment of those in the farming sector by banks and it published a report with 27 recommendations at the conclusion of a year's work that involved 115 submissions and 11 public hearings. These recommendations covered areas including but not limited to education to improve financial literacy; changes to the Code of Banking Practice administered by the Australian Bankers' Association; tighter regulation of insolvency practitioners so that they disclose their costs and provide monthly reports; funding for rural counsellors to be involved; and rules related to the manner in which documents reflecting the financial situation of a farmer should only be altered by a farmer or their representative and not a bank. The final recommendation of this committee's report was for the Hayne Royal Commission to consider all of the evidence that had been presented to the committee during its year-long look at the banks and their conduct towards those in the rural sector.

THE NATIONALS CUT LOOSE – ANOTHER BILL

The then deputy prime minister Barnaby Joyce was found to be a dual citizen by the High Court of Australia as his father was born in New Zealand. This forced Joyce back on the election trail to reclaim his seat of New England, which he did with an increased majority. He also managed to do so without his infidelities to his wife Natalie hitting mainstream media outlets despite rumours that Vicki Campion and Joyce had become romantic. These personal and electoral distractions meant that Joyce, the political master of spin, was unable to control his national party colleagues who were getting restless as far as investigating the banking sector was concerned. Senator Barry O'Sullivan had begun to agitate for a second vote for the establishment of a parliamentary commission of inquiry into the financial services sector. A Bill was prepared for debate in the Senate and it was similar to the initial Bill introduced in March by Whish-Wilson but there were differences. The pressure from the Coalition partner was mounting but the government was still resisting the call for a royal commission. The absence of Joyce meant that the government was incapable of keeping the National party members in line. Their determination for an inquiry as well as the support for one from other parties in the Senate would ultimately cause the government to take action. The so-called iron law of arithmetic kicked in and the Liberals in the coalition feared embarrassment on the floor of the parliament if another bill for a parliamentary commission of inquiry was to get up.

THE SECOND LAST DOMINO FALLS

The ultimate source of resistance to a royal commission into the financial services sector were the banks themselves and they directly lobbied the government to institute an inquiry when it became apparent that the political winds within Canberra were heading in a direction that could result in a parliamentary commission of inquiry that had been threatened by the National Party. They were the second last domino to fall and two letters were sent to Morrison to put forward the case for a royal commission despite the fact that the banks themselves repeatedly argued against it. The direct appeal to the Australian Treasurer was a sign that the banks feared a parliamentary commission of inquiry that would have its terms of reference drafted by parliamentarians that had been agitating for a royal commission for some time. Former NAB chairman Ken Henry had discussions with Morrison prior to the sending of the first draft of correspondence attached to an email sent on 29 November 2017. The draft was largely consistent in both tone and intent with the final, signed version sent to Morrison the following day – on which the government announced its intention to convene a royal commission of inquiry. The banks said:

We are writing to you as the leaders of Australia's major banks. In light of the latest wave of speculation about a parliamentary commission of inquiry into the banking and finance sector, we believe it is now imperative for the Australian Government to act decisively to deliver certainty to Australia's financial services sector, our customers and the community.

Our banks have consistently argued the view that further inquiries into the sector, including a Royal Commission, are unwarranted. They are costly and unnecessary distractions at a time when the finance sector faces significant challenges and disruption from technology and growing global macroeconomic uncertainty.

However, it is now in the national interest for the political uncertainty to end. It is hurting confidence in our financial services system, including in offshore markets, and has diminished trust and respect for our sector and people. It also risks undermining the critical perception that our banks are unquestionably strong.

The letter from the banking goliaths confirmed the close-knit liaison on the matter of inquiries between the Federal Government and the financial services sector. This was not a surrender by the banks, however, because they would have in their own mind snatched victory from the jaws of defeat. They would have known the weak spots in their operations but the extent of the weakness or vulnerabilities and, indeed, manipulations by their own employees would be revealed only under the harsh spotlight of the royal commission that was to come. It would not be unreasonable to conclude that the banks were participants in the task of laying the tracks upon which the Hayne express was to run.

THE LIBERAL SURRENDER – OR WAS IT?

Turnbull and Morrison finally gave in to the pressure for a royal commission to be held into the institutions that have colloquially but not always affectionately been called 'bastards' on 30 November 2017. A press conference represented a final backdown from the steadfast opposition to a royal commission by the government, parts of the financial services sector and commentators in the media. The National Party's rebelliousness and the banking sector's defensiveness both achieved something that countless tales of woe on television and in print media failed to do – the calling of an inquiry that was to spend no more than a year examining a series of targeted areas in order to determine how best to correct behaviours that were both seen as being below community expectations and also appeared to teeter on a knife's edge where legality was concerned.

The then prime minister and the then treasurer spent time during the press conference ensuring that they talked up the stability of Australia's financial system and branded the royal commission as something regrettable that needed to happen, which made it sound like the judicial equivalent of preparing for Christmas dinner with the in-laws, a visit to the dentist or a journey home from the office at peak time on a clogged freeway. Each of these may be regrettable, but necessary. 'But the nature of political events,' Morrison said, 'means the national economic interest is now served by taking what I describe as a regrettable but necessary action.' The then treasurer consulted with regulators who agreed that the action was 'a regrettable but necessary course of action now to take control, given the uncertainty, disruption, and damage being done by political events'. The banks – the organisations to be probed by the royal commission – confirmed this to the treasurer in the aforementioned correspondence. It should be clear, however, that the calling of a royal commission was more than just being 'regrettable but necessary'. It was a final acknowledgement that the government had failed to persuade a broad range of stakeholders that reviews of financial institutions and similar organisations by bodies such as the parliamentary committees, the Productivity Commission, reviews by the regulators and others were fit for purpose and would deliver the necessary change over time. The Turnbull cabinet had only one card left in its hand to play and an impatient, irritated, angry mob of consumers and political opponents forced them to lay it on the table, turn it over and admit defeat.

Turnbull's performance at the media conference was also laced with references to the commission being a regret, but also being necessary. It was also firmly rooted in the belief that only the government would be able to create a terms of reference that would be responsible, comprehensive, appropriately resourced and chaired by a 'distinguished former or serving judicial officer'. 'Now, this will not be an open-ended commission. It's not going to put capitalism on trial, as some people in the Parliament would prefer,' Turnbull pointedly said. 'The Terms of Reference will ensure a responsible but comprehensive investigation into how financial institutions have dealt with cases of misconduct in the past, and whether those examples expose issues in terms of the cultural and governance issues in terms of the regulation and supervision of the industry.' He told the assembled media that banks, wealth managers, superannuation providers and insurers would be captured by the terms of reference in order to make it comprehensive. Recommendations related to compensation in individual cases would be outside the scope of the Commissioner's remit but, Turnbull said, recommendations dealing with making the financial systems the 'most competitive, transparent and accountable in the world' would be a focus.

Turnbull said that Australians had many things to be proud of where the country's financial system was concerned. He noted that the global financial crisis should remind taxpayers of the fact that the financial services sector in this country did not suffer as much damage as financial institutions in other jurisdictions. This did not mean that there were not trust issues and Turnbull observed that consumers, small businesses, farmers, shareholders and other stakeholders need to have confidence in the banking sector.

The then prime minister said he felt the royal commission would end uncertainty and speculation and that it would be conducted in a manner that would 'safeguard the integrity of our banks and our other financial institutions thereby ensuring Australia's confidence and trust in this critical industry is well founded'.

Politics, Scott Morrison argued during the 30 November press conference, was the threat to the national interest where the banks and the future of the financial system was concerned. The then treasurer argued politics was driving the process of a royal commission. 'Well politics will continue to damage the national economic interest if we allow politics to continue to drive this process. By taking control through a royal commission, that is something that was in the ambit of the government, then I think we can provide that certainty that Australian families, that Australian businesses, that international markets and others are seeking,' he told the assembled media on the day the government hoisted the white flag of surrender. 'It's regrettable but necessary. It's regrettable that the politics, principally, with the politicking of the Opposition has led to this, but that said, we will stand up for the national economic interest of Australians jobs.'

Scott Morrison – the treasurer to whom the banking sector wrote asking for a royal commission – would end up being the country's prime minister when both the interim and final reports from the royal commission his government had resisted were handed down.

HAYNE VERSUS THE BANKS:
THE OPENING SHOT

||||||||||||||||||||||||||||||||||||||||||||||||||

'Instead, as I see it, we will have to proceed by reference to case studies and examples, with a view to identifying the kinds of misconduct that have occurred, why it has occurred, what should have been and what was the response to discovering the misconduct, and then what follows from those conclusions and observations.'

COMMISSIONER KENNETH HAYNE

'A confidentiality or non-disparagement clause in an agreement will not act as a reasonable excuse against production in answer to a notice to produce or a summons.'

COMMISSIONER KENNETH HAYNE

THE BIG FOUR BANKS may have been at the centre of orchestrating the royal commission but that does not mean they and their fellow financial services companies were at all keen to part with information in a hurry as requested by Commissioner Hayne in letters sent to major players late in 2017. A preliminary hearing was held on 12 February 2018 to outline the terms of references of the Commission as well as the progress that the team assembled for the royal commission had made. Not everyone involved approached by Commissioner Hayne and his team chose to play nice and the chief inquisitor made clear that it was taking a while to get some information from the entities that were in his sights. The commissioner had sent letters to a range of entities, which included the major banks, asking them a series of questions that were based on terms of reference. Those financial service entities receiving correspondence from the commissioner were asked to take the commissioner through a series of issues that included the forms of misconduct that the royal commission was required to investigate. What the Hayne team effectively asked people to do was draw out examples of poor conduct engaged in by their own staff irrespective of the rank held within the financial institution. This amounted to the largest companies in Australia engaging in an orgy of self-incrimination before the royal commission began to look more deeply at specific case studies.

The requests were responded to by large financial services entities but some of them failed to deal with the request as Commissioner Hayne required. 'Examination of those responses showed that in important respects, some large industry participants had sought to respond by giving examples of misconduct or conduct they identified as falling short of community standards and expectations rather than, as my original request had asked, by specifying the nature, extent and effect of the conduct they had identified,' the Commissioner explained. 'I therefore wrote to some of those large respondents on Friday 2 February asking each to give more specific information about misconduct identified by that entity over the last five years, and in addition, I asked some of them to amplify some of the information provided in their original responses.'

The Commissioner told those present at the initial hearing that a request for 10 years' worth of information was made on 15 December 2017 with responses arriving from the banks by January 29. 'That a request for details of events of misconduct as defined in the terms of reference identified during the last five years cannot be met within the time sought, even though the initial request for that information was made approximately two months ago, is itself a matter to which further attention may have to be given,' the Commissioner observed. 'Whether it is will be a matter for debate at a later time.'

Work done by the commission in its early days also involved asking for and then analysing submissions from members of the public that had experienced misconduct or what they thought was misconduct by banks and other financial institutions. It was acknowledged in this preliminary hearing by Commissioner Hayne that members of the public that had been victims of misconduct would want to use the royal commission to get recognition, consideration and some degree of public disclosure of their case. But that there was no way in which the inquiry would be able to consider every individual case. 'We will have to proceed by reference to case studies and examples with a view to identifying the kinds of misconduct, what should have been and what was the response to discovering the misconduct, and what follows from those conclusions,' Commissioner Hayne said. The inquiry would spend more time, the commission's chief said, dissecting the reasons for misconduct and how best to avoid such misconduct taking place again.

A concern that had become apparent in getting the royal commission off the ground was the potential for banks and other institutions to attempt to stop clients from providing submissions or evidence of misconduct by relying on confidentiality clauses contained in agreements entered into by both parties for remediation. There are other areas in which confidentiality is of some legal consequence. People have employment agreements, settlement agreements related to unfair dismissals and other agreements that do contain non-disparagement or 'gag' clauses. These clauses are used deliberately to try and give the parties that have been in dispute with each other the opportunity to start afresh either in a new career without the fear of past mistakes or business relationship breakdowns interfering with a personal or professional life reset. While these arrangements may assist in drawing a line in the sand in individual circumstances, concern was expressed about the ability of the royal commission to get the necessary information from those that feel they are affected by confidentiality clauses. Responding to a notice of summons related to appear before or to produce information to the royal commission would not be in conflict with confidentiality clauses, Commissioner Hayne told those assembled for his first address. There was also a caution to those that might attempt to threaten legal action against people who had sought to reveal more information about misconduct to which they either fell victim or saw unfold when employed by an institution. 'Further – and this is very important – under section 6M of the Royal Commissions Act, if a witness gives evidence or produces a document under a notice or summons, no injury can be done to that person,' Commissioner Hayne explained. 'Suing the person would almost certainly fall within that prohibition.' The royal commission's legal team had also contemplated the circumstances where an entity would seek legal redress of some form against a client, member of the public or whistle blower before the commission had officially kicked off consideration of bad things banks had done. It was flagged to those present at the hearing that there were two possible outcomes. Compulsory powers to seize information would be used by the commission. '[The] very fact that an institution sought to inhibit or prevent the disclosure of the information would excite the closest attention not only to the lawfulness of that conduct by the institution, but also to what were the institution's motives for seeking to prevent the commission having that information,' Commissioner Hayne observed.

SHOCK AND ORR BEGINS

Senior Counsel assisting Rowena Orr QC, the lawyer who quickly won widespread admiration for her rapier-like interrogation of bank executives, spoke for the first time at this preliminary hearing with her primary purpose being to outline the work program of the commission and the manner in which hearings would proceed. The commission, she said, would publish a range of documents that would support the work of the commission as well as seek submissions related to the specific topics the commission was considering during a specific round of hearings. Orr provided some insight into matters of concern that were being raised by those providing submissions for consideration by the commission. She said that 84 per cent of submissions received by the commission by 12 February 2018 had focused on misconduct that fell below community standards and expectations. 'Forty per cent relate to culture and governance practices of financial services entities and 35 per cent relate to the effectiveness of redress for consumers. Some themes have already emerged from the public submissions,' Orr said. Submissions lodged by members of the public covered familiar themes that were already on the public record in evidence given by victims of misconduct before various parliamentary committees. Evidence was received by Orr and her team that related to financial institutions executing financial advice based on false documentation, provision of inappropriate financial advice, lending practices that left much to be desired as well as insurance claim processing delays.

The question of corporate culture within financial institutions was a theme within the submission. This area was again one that was traversed in parliamentary committees such as the House of Representatives and Senate Economics Committees that had looked at the financial services sector in detail in preceding years, which included the forensic examination of the decline of integrity in the management of aspects of the financial planning business in the Commonwealth Bank. 'These submissions refer to matters such as incentive-based remuneration, which is regarded as encouraging such representatives to secure an outcome that is not necessarily appropriate for the consumer, such as a loan for an amount in excess of the amount sought,' Orr observed. 'They also refer to Commissions payable to a financial advisor by a financial institution for referring its products to the consumer. In relation to the effectiveness of redress, we have seen a large number of submissions that express frustration and concern about the time taken and effort required to navigate the internal and external dispute resolution frameworks that apply to financial services entities.' These submissions would end up being used as the basis for determining what case studies ought to be examined during the year-long inquiry into the rorts, rip offs and deceptions used by financial institutions when dealing with their clients.

THE MAKING OF A WHISTLE BLOWER

||||||||||||||||||||||||||||||||||||||||||||||||

'More than $22 million in compensation was paid to clients who had received inappropriate financial advice from two Commonwealth Financial Planning advisers, Mr Don Nguyen and Mr Anthony Awkar.'

ROWENA ORR QC, SENIOR COUNSEL ASSISTING,
HAYNE ROYAL COMMISSION

'The only problem with that, mate, is that ASIC is shit. They'll never do anything.'

ANONYMOUS CBA WHISTLE BLOWER

'I have a difficulty with any professionals with a fiduciary duty where you are also making them salesmen.'

JEFF MORRIS, CBA WHISTLE BLOWER

FORMER COMMONWEALTH BANK financial adviser Jeff Morris is the whistle blower largely credited for starting the brush fire that caused politicians to pay attention to the problems in the financial services sector that was later to become a bushfire that would not be extinguished until the Turnbull Government called a royal commission. An experienced financial professional, Morris had clearly seen better days before he stumbled across conduct at the bank that caused him to complain to authorities because inertia caused by financial self-interest within the bank caused people to either avert their gaze or be actively complicit in covering up misconduct that would later be the subject of and also become a fixture at a series of parliamentary inquiries designed to try and let more than just a slight shard of light into the dark and corrupted corners of the Commonwealth Bank's financial planning operation. Morris walked the path all too often walked by whistle blowers: the minute he broke ranks from the Commonwealth Bank was the moment the dirt machine was switched on. Parliamentarians were encouraged to disregard the evidence of an insider that had blown open the practices within the bank and also the inaction of a regulator that was warned about the activities of individuals that fell outside standard of conduct from financial advisers that consumers were entitled to expect.

The problem for the bank in briefing politicians and others against Morris was their target was not your garden variety disgruntled employee that packed no punch in terms of qualifications, corporate experience or integrity. Morris, an economics and law graduate from the University of Sydney, had a lifetime of work in the financial services under his belt before he walked into the financial planning arm of 'Which Bank' for what he expected was going to be a quieter period in his career. He is a Certified Financial Planner and had worked in the financial services sector since 1985. The roll call of the positions he held in organisations indicates that that he was a trusted professional in the financial services sector. One Australian bank employed him as their corporate tax manager. He was an executive manager in the CBA's private bank and also rose to hold a position of Vice President of Bankers' Trust. Morris' career as a financial adviser began when he joined actuaries Towers Perrin in 1990. 'I have expertise in the fields of financial planning, taxation law, superannuation and corporate remuneration and a deep knowledge of investment markets and the funds management industry,' Morris told the Senate committee inquiring into the performance of the corporate regulator during an intense inquiry that involved a deep dive into the operations of the Commonwealth Bank. His involvement with Commonwealth Financial Planning commenced in 2008 and it was to define his financial planning career in a very different, very public and often stressful light.

UNCOMMON WEALTH AT THE CBA?

It was not long after he began working as part of the financial planning team that Morris began to notice irregularities and inappropriate behaviours amongst some of his colleagues at the bank with one colleague, 'Dodgy Don' Nguyen, getting a disproportionate amount of Morris' attention. Evidence tendered to the Senate Committee inquiry highlighted Nguyen's aggressive pursuit of new clients across a series of branches. He was instrumental in creating a scheme whereby he would pay tellers. Nguyen was coming to the attention of the CBA's financial planning team because it appeared he was cutting corners in process as well as making under the table payments to bank tellers so they referred financial planning clients directly to him. It was a revenue rich vein Nguyen was after and it was clear that Nguyen had found willing accomplices who were happy to direct traffic Nguyen's way for a spotter's fee. Morris described Nguyen as a 'ferocious business writer' who sold the notion of investment returns to his clients with 'no risk' in submissions to the Senate Committee. 'He sold off recent strong historical returns. He also worked in a hurry and only wanted to spend the minimum time to get the business, so he didn't want to waste his time or confuse or create doubt in client's minds by explaining concepts like risk to them or going through a risk profiling exercise,' Morris said. 'He also had a penchant for charging high ongoing service fees [whilst not actually delivering any service] which were much easier to justify [or more likely to be overlooked by clients] with aggressive portfolios delivering high returns.' Nguyen appeared to use this method to quickly build his book of clients. Nguyen may have genuinely believed the approach was best for his clients, Morris said, and that he saw his method also as generating commissions for himself.

HARVESTING CLIENTS, HARVESTING COMMISSIONS

How did Nguyen's method of harvesting clients for his own client book work? The 39-page written statement that formed a part of a series of documents submitted by Morris to the Senate inquiry in 2013 chronicles the Nguyen saga, which was only one illustration of the kinds of behaviours that would drive the push for a royal commission over a three-year period. Morris began a stint as the branch financial planner in Mosman in April 2008. It did not take long for Morris to notice the curious and concerning behaviour of his colleague. One bank employee saw Nguyen talking with a former ABC newsreader, but that person was not known to be a client attached to Nguyen's client portfolio. Morris had found out that Nguyen had told the client he was the new branch planner for Mosman but also that the client was 'horrified by Don Nguyen and his proposals and had no intention of dealing with him'. It was also discovered that Nguyen had put through a batch of what Morris describes as 'self-generated' referrals without those clients knowing or meeting with him. The impact of putting a client through as 'self-generated' was that Nguyen got an incentive payment for appearing to pull that business into the bank himself. This was a part of the Nguyen's 'under the table' scheme in which bank tellers would direct client traffic to Nguyen. Evidence provided to the Senate committee noted that the 'cash backhanders', as Morris tagged them, had several impacts internally. So-called self-generated referrals were not entered into a system as a branch referral, which denied the retail branch credit for generating business to which it was entitled, and also it cheated the customer out of getting access to one of the bank's senior planners.

What caused Morris to grow more concerned was the fact that there were 11 sets of client files that were missing. These files belonged to the largest clients that Morris had inherited and one of those customers 'stormed into the branch angry that Don Nguyen had rung her from Chatswood, telling her he was looking at her file as he spoke and claiming [falsely] to be her new financial planner'. The customer did not want to meet with a planner in Chatswood but wanted to deal with a planner based in Mosman. These missing files and the poaching of Mosman clients was reported by Morris to the financial planning manager. A conversation between the manager and Nguyen followed with the manager telling Morris that Nguyen would not try to take clients from the Mosman branch. It appeared, however, that there were 11 client files that had vanished. Nguyen denied having them and the manager accepted this assertion. 'Normally I would have thought this would be a major compliance issue,' Morris said. 'To this day I don't know what happened to those client files.'

The new Mosman branch financial planner asked why Nguyen was not being sacked for dishonesty and he was told Nguyen, the rainmaker, was a 'big writer' of business, protected by those higher up and untouchable. 'Flabbergasted, I could only reply that maybe I didn't know the politics but in any other organisation I'd ever worked at Don would be sacked for stealing client files and brazenly lying to clients,' Morris said.

There were other colleagues, however, that briefed Morris on the background of 'Dodgy Don', which is how Nguyen was known inside the bank. It was made clear to Morris that 'Dodgy Don' was a protected species because he brought a large amount of business in and the culture of the place meant that the equation of sales equalling revenue then equalling bonuses as difficult for people to ignore. 'The sales of 'Dodgy Don' and other crooked planners [and for that matter in-house lenders and external mortgage brokers as well] did not just directly drive their own bonuses/remuneration but also those of all the tiers of managers above them,' Morris said. 'Understanding the behavioural impact of this remuneration structure for all the managers in the chain above the financial planners is a key aspect to understanding what happened here and what continues to happen in the industry.'

Nguyen's method of doing business, Morris noted, was not particularly novel. There was a system and a culture built around it that ensured those engaged in looser financial planning practices were rewarded and protected by Commonwealth Bank managers with something to gain. Nguyen wrote business. Nguyen made money and was rewarded. Those to whom Nguyen reported were also financially rewarded for their division's success. Killing the goose laying the golden eggs was not exactly on the agenda for the management in the financial planning arm. Morris told the Senate committee examining the Commonwealth Bank's financial planning regime that rogue planners survived because the financial planning business enabled them but this was also done under 'ASIC's benevolent gaze'.

Compliance functions such as the audits of practitioner files within the financial planning arm were also corrupted by this sales-ridden culture. These audits were conducted by people with the skills and the ability to find errors in the documentation and conduct of planners but the process still favoured some of the individuals that were hoovering the cash into the financial planning practice's coffers that stimulated the generation of commissions and bonuses further up the chain of command. 'Dodgy Don' Nguyen had failed several internal audits of his files but senior management intervened to protect the rainmaker on several occasions, according to the evidence from Morris, but there was a time when Nguyen's activities caught up with him. He was suspended for a period and compliance auditors got their hands on additional files with Nguyen out of the office. 'This revealed that segments of the fact finds were common to many clients – even photocopied. All clients, even in vastly different circumstances, had the same aggressive risk profiles. An astonishing proportion also "specifically requested 50% in [listed property trusts]".'

What Morris saw as being a greater concern was the fact that Nguyen was promoted to a senior planner in the network rather than being shunted off-stage left in the interests of protecting clients and the bank in the long term. This occurred despite the number of complaints being generated following Nguyen's advice.

Suspension in 2008 did not stop 'Dodgy Don' Nguyen doing business and this became apparent when more missing files were discovered around June 2009 when Jan Braund, a client who had seen Nguyen, was given to Morris. A servicing planner that worked beneath Nguyen would bring files over to the suspended financial planner who operated from a nearby shopping centre. The servicing planner also assisted Nguyen to sanitise files when the heat was turned up. '[The files] may have been in his car boot so he could see clients while suspended. Or they may have never existed,' Morris said in his Senate committee submission. 'Or the missing files may have been some of the files that had been found non-compliant by CFP's Compliance Department in September 2008, that Nguyen simply hadn't had time to clean up.' Nguyen saw Jan Braund, who along with her husband had trusted the bank with $1.2 million, at a shopping centre while he was on suspension. The suspended planner sought to explain away losses in her portfolio but Braund had stopping trusting Nguyen. 'Jan had been having trouble with Don Nguyen and CFP for over a year. Her complaint that he had failed to act on her instructions in late 2007 to "safeguard" her portfolio was initially dismissed by CBA in the most condescending and insulting terms,' said Morris. 'Only after several debilitating years of conflict did they finally pay up.' Braund spoke to Morris for the first time on the phone from New Zealand and told him that she had been 'fobbed off' by the financial planning team manager and customer service staff. Braund also noted in conversation with Morris that she 'knew Nguyen had been forging her instructions using a blank piece of paper with her signature on it'. Braund told Morris that nobody took her allegation of her signature being forged seriously. Morris told her otherwise and gave her the details of CBA Group Security. Braund duly sent a fax detailing the forgery allegations on 2 July 2009. Morris searched through Braund's client file but there was no blank piece of paper with her signature in there. 'By this time Nguyen had eight months to sanitise his files since we had tipped off ASIC,' Morris said. Braund was given a full copy of her client file by Morris so that she would know what the bank had about her at the point in time she was formally complaining about the conduct.

Braund's access to her full file meant that the she and her representatives, Financial Resolution Australia, were able to demand that the CBA produce the full file that was handed over to CBA Group Security by Morris. The CBA ended up agreeing to a larger than normal payout in the case of Braund because, Morris said, they were less than keen on handing over her client file. 'CBA had already suppressed a key document, a paraplanning instruction, helpful to her argument, from the documents they handed over under terms of the ASIC sponsored compensation scheme,' Morris revealed. 'The full file has never been handed over by CBA. Under pressure, even from ASIC in the end, to hand over these documents, CBA suddenly increased their offer from the $330,000 it had crept up to over the years to $880,000 in August 2012.' Morris said that it the increase in compensation was to avoid releasing the client file and doing any forensic work to determine whether her complaint about a forged signature had substance.

Braund was not the only client that raised alarm bells for Morris in his quest to try and get things put right for people who were seeing what they thought was a solid plan for their retirement. The implications of this sales driven culture had a real cost for clients who had stories that were difficult for Morris to hear. It caused him to strengthen his resolve to tell the world about the problems within the CBA. 'The year of birth of one distressed client that I spoke to was 1917,' Morris said. 'He was an elderly man; he told me he was on the Burma railway. All of his money had been put into this mortgage fund – it was very irresponsible to have put it all there – just so a planner could earn some revenue and so some managers could get a bonus. Then they froze the fund and these people were left high and dry.' It wasn't just the fact that the funds were parked in a mortgage fund. It was also, Morris said, what the bank continued to siphon from these accounts in terms of fees and charges at a time when it was difficult to get clients to buy into the share market because they were spooked by the global financial crisis that was unfolding. Morris told the Senate Committee that planners were told to 'hose down' the clients and try to get them to not complain about the financial advice they had received.

MONEY FOR NOTHING THE CBA WAY

Morris provided the Senate committee probing the Commonwealth Bank case study with details of how financial planners made money for no service at all. The sleight of hand, according to Morris, would only be noticed if customers were aware that the investment platform that they were using for their investment services was one they could manage on their own without the assistance of a financial planner. While there were fees disclosed in the statement of advice that investors must be given under law, an important fact was omitted. 'What was not disclosed in the Statements of Advice was the fact that, since the Colonial First State platforms were open to direct investment by individuals without going through an adviser, it was possible for individuals to invest directly without incurring any adviser fees,' Morris said. 'On the contrary, the Statements of Advice gave the misleading impression that both the upfront and ongoing CFPL fees were the price of entry for accessing the CFS platforms.' The whistle blower asserted that most clients would believe that they could only get at these products if they paid the fee that was disclosed. Financial planners were encouraged to ensure they did not highlight the fact that investors were not obliged to pay for advice if they chose only to control their own investments via the Commonwealth platforms.

Morris described the advice fee that was taken as a 'straightforward clipping of the coupon' that produced what was recurring income to the financial planning arm. This was made more insidious by the fact that there was no enforcement of what Morris called a prescribed standard of advice. In other words, the client rip off was institutionalised. Less curious and pliant customers bore the brunt of costs for nothing. 'It was well understood by the planners that you were not allowed, on pain of dismissal, to tell clients they didn't have to pay this fee if they didn't want to,' Morris explained. 'Massive business revenues had been built up over the years by charging clients this ongoing fee without providing any services in return and without any intention of doing so.' Morris estimated that hundreds of millions were taken from clients using this sleight of hand and chiefs in the financial planning arm of the Commonwealth Bank were adamant that the truth about their 'bundled' service should not be told.

A financial planning unit compliance manager presented to advisers in June 2011 and sought to reinforce the fees for no service regime. One adviser asked whether the optional nature of the fees for advisory services could be discussed with customers. 'You're not allowed to tell clients that they don't have to pay this fee. You tell them what the services are and what the fee is,' the compliance manager stated. 'If they specifically ask you whether they have to pay the fee then you can tell them "no", but you can't volunteer that information.' It is reported by Morris in a submission to the Senate committee that he asked whether planners cannot 'fully and properly' explain the conditions in the statement of advice to clients. The compliance manager 'snapped' and told Morris that 'you explain that fee to your clients the same way you have for the past three years and if you have a problem with that talk to [redacted] about it'. It was clear to Morris that divergence from the orders from above would lead to discipline at best and, at worst, likely termination of employment. This was not an isolated attempt to reinforce a culture of selling products without fully disclosing that certain fees could be sidestepped by the client if they wanted to drive their investment process themselves.

MORPHING INTO WHISTLE BLOWER

It was 'Dodgy Don' Nguyen's conduct and the conduct of those executives that sought to protect Nguyen that forced Morris' hand and caused him to turn whistle blower. There were three planners including Morris who were deeply concerned about the practices that were being engaged in at the CBA's financial planning arm and each of them wanted in some way to ensure that wrongs were eventually put right. The trio decided to call themselves the 'Three Ferrets' and lodge an account of activities at the CBA with the corporate regulator. This account was sent in anonymously because the three whistle blowers were concerned for their own safety in speaking out about the practices in which the Commonwealth Bank was engaged. Morris told the parliamentary committee in 2014 that there was also a concern about the ability of the corporate regulator to keep the knowledge of complainants to themselves and one ASIC officer, Adrian Borchok, told them at a meeting with ASIC on 24 February 2010 that the whistle blower protection 'is not worth much'. The 'Three Ferrets' knew that their jobs would be at risk at the outset if they proceeded with their activities on what had been going on at the Commonwealth Bank. They proceeded to do so anyway.

The three men decided to write a comprehensive outline of the problems within the CBA financial planning concern that included the manner in which Nguyen behaved and also the way in which the hierarchy sought to cover the situation up. The report to ASIC highlighted the fact that there were CBA staff that had described the scenario as a 'conspiracy' to ensure that clients were dealt with individually on issues related to inappropriate advice and that there would be no scope for people to be able to 'join the dots' and thereby create grounds for a class action the bank may find difficult to defend. It is described in the letter from the three whistle blowers to ASIC as a conspiracy to defraud clients of proper compensation. What was the outcome of three planners putting themselves out on a limb? It would be wrong to say that the outcome was nothing because the bank's chief writer of financial planning business had two assistants getting busy readying files for external examination. 'After sending this fax we expected ASIC to turn up with a warrant to seize the files. We had after all mentioned the need to secure them as they were being "cleaned up" by Don Nguyen and his two assistants,' Morris said. However, as the days passed with no sign of a fire breathing regulator on the doorstep, we decided to follow up ASIC by email. Weeks turned into months. Email followed email. ASIC said they were investigating. But if that were so, why hadn't they seized the files?' Morris' main submission to the Senate committee investigating ASIC's performance noted that the bank knew of the problems and that clients were being told that the reason for losses in their investments was the global financial crisis. In fact, the bank itself was praising Nguyen for writing so much business. Morris recalled that Nguyen missed a year-end get together with staff to chase down more dollars.

'[Nguyen] missed the team's Christmas Party in 2008 – barefoot bowls – because he and his two servicing planners were busy trying to stitch up a 93-year-old with $1.6 million to invest for a $32,000 [2% flat] advice fee,' Morris said. 'It goes without saying that no financial planner with a shred of decency to them would have contemplated acting in this way.' The managers highlighted Nguyen's entrepreneurial nature to the other staff. The bigger the deal, the bigger the commission and – given the way the CBA's scheme worked at the time – the bigger the pay-off for those further up the chain as recognition for their success in hitting their financial targets.

The lack of visible action from the corporate regulator meant that the whistle blowers needed another form of leverage. They eventually decided to go to the media and the choice target was the industry-related news site, *Investor Daily*. One of the 'ferrets' knew journalist Darin Tyson-Chan, and Tyson-Chan published the first of the articles that dealt with the failure of ASIC to deal speedily with the complaint on 18 May 2009. A second article, which was let loose into the wild on 25 May 2009, named Nguyen as a central focus of the controversy. Other articles followed these two and described the facts as they were reported to the corporate regulator. There was no hint of urgency from the corporate regulator to resolve issues following publication, Morris said, but the bank reacted as if a fire had been lit. Nguyen vanished from sight two days after the article naming him was published for what was to be his second suspension in as many years. The Commonwealth Bank got its internal investigators at CBA Group

Security involved to get further details from staff about Nguyen and his activities. This created the opportunity for Morris to blow the whistle on the protection racket being run for Nguyen by the financial planning business.

It was on 2 June 2009 that Morris had an interview with CBA Group Security and he told the Senate in his written submission that he did not reveal everything he knew about the problems within the financial planning arm. He focused on the activities specifically surrounding Nguyen because Morris knew 'it was apparent they were, at that initial stage, primarily on a Ferret hunt to catch the leakers to *Investor Daily*'. CBA Group Security asked Morris whether he knew about the purported suspension of Nguyen in 2008. 'It seemed that they hadn't got the truth about this from CFP Management. They asked me how many people knew. I explained that the whole team certainly knew but many people outside the team also knew; that the 'Dodgy Don' sobriquet was well known in the business,' Morris said. 'After some further discussion about the *Investor Daily* articles they asked me how the team felt when Don was promoted after he'd been suspended. I said we were flabbergasted.' Morris also told his interviewers that there was a conspiracy related to avoiding the payment of compensation for those individuals that received inappropriate advice that caused the amount they had invested to nosedive at the most inopportune time of their lives.

INDUSTRIAL SCALE DOCUMENT FRAUD

There still appeared to be an emphasis on finding out who leaked the detail of Nguyen's financial planning activities to *Investor Daily*. While more digging was being done to find three ferrets, an email from a 'Mallord' describing the Nguyen controversy in some detail found its way to senior management at the bank. One person, with name redacted in Morris' written evidence, was accused during an interview, which was taped, of conspiring with Morris and another individual to get Nguyen. Questions asked during the CBA Group

Security interrogation of one individual also went to the amount of Liquid Paper in Nguyen's files, whether he was the sender of the diary note and also whether he was the mysterious 'Mallord' who had sent the email with details of the Nguyen protection racket.

CBA Group Security eventually produced a report but it, according to Morris, appeared to have been buried in the 'CBA Chamber of Secrets'. While Nguyen was allowed to resign from the bank, there was little respite for the clients who were still being refused the compensation they deserved. Another financial planner was brought in to carry on where Nguyen left off. His task was to keep the clients from complaining with the financial crisis – and not poor advice – being the favoured culprit. Morris also noticed that there was an off-site location that was somewhat secretive and it appeared to involve a lot of files in boxes getting taken away. This was known as 'Project Hartnett', Morris said, and it appeared to pick up where Nguyen left off with clients' files.

'Strangely, although the floor at [the Chatswood offices] was only 10% occupied at most, separate premises were set up for the bulk of the Hartnett team, said in one internal adviser briefing by [redacted] to number as many as 40 people at one time,' Morris said. 'The secrecy surrounding Project Hartnett, the file sanitation by Nguyen that had gone before it, the sheer number and the demeanour of people working on it and the seemingly unnecessary and expensive off-site location, all added to the impression that skulduggery was afoot.' Morris said there was a procession of men in suits taking boxes of client files from the Chatswood office to the off-site location.

Morris had concluded that the people working on Project Harnett were doing more than just calculating compensation. He had come to a view that they were actually working on the files to clean them up en masse. 'There was a large team of people working on those files from June 2009 to March 2010. They were not just 'reviewing' the files to pay people compensation, because they weren't really interested in paying compensation at that stage, these people were working on the files,' Morris said. 'Most of this and I suspect the more clandestine work took place in an office in the Sydney CBD set up for the purpose.' Morris said that there were some people in the Chatswood office that were working in lockstep with the planner assigned to deceive clients but the main work related to the files moving in and out of the secret city-based location was done by contract staff and permanent staff on rotation.

A servicing planner and paraplanner involved in doctoring client files as a part of Project Hartnett told him that the files were being rewritten and recompiled so that the advice documents retrofitted the investments in which client funds had been placed. This process of 'reverse engineering' would enable the bank to deny any claim of inappropriate advice because it would seem to the untrained eye that the client had agreed to go into an aggressive investment portfolio and other documents would look like they supported the conclusion. This was industrial scale document fraud designed primarily to avoid compensation payouts wherever possible. The paraplanner, according to Morris, appeared clearly uncomfortable about what he was being told to do. 'Even knowing what I knew at the time, I frankly found this hard to believe and it seemed inconceivable to me that an organisation like CBA could be this stupid,' Morris said. There was evidence presented by clients that advice documents were altered with different dates and details. Differences in dates of documents were explained away by people at the bank as being a normal occurrence when a document is printed on a date other than the first time the document was signed. Morris said that clients such as Robyn Blanch were lied to by bank staff. 'The opposite is, in fact, the case: the original Statement of Advice can always be reprinted and will retain the original date as long as the document has not been altered.' The bank was caught out because Blanch had a copy of the original documentation and was capable of demonstrating the alterations that were made to the original advice-related documents.

Braund and Merilyn Swan, the daughter of Blanch, gave evidence during the Senate committee hearings in 2014 probing ASIC's performance. The evidence of both aligns with the account presented by Morris while being focused on the impact of CBA's services on them as individuals. Swan said the CBA denied there was any problem with the advice provided by Nguyen. 'They then reported that they had lost my mother's file and then sent my parents copies of fraudulently altered and falsified documents that CBA management had manufactured to convince my parents that they were responsible for choosing high-risk investments,' Swan said. 'These documents include a fraudulent statement of advice and a second financial needs analysis, complete with forged signature, fraudulent changes to my mother's contract made after it was signed on 10 May 2007, and a falsified table purported to be extracted from the original statement of advice of 3 March 2007.' Swan told the Senate Committee that the bank never responded to a submission sent to the Financial Ombudsman's Service and there was no contact from the bank to tell her parents scope existed for a review of their settlement once the Commonwealth Bank entered into an enforceable undertaking with the corporate regulator. Braund told the Senate committee that she ultimately did receive a copy of her file from the bank but that there was a critical document that was missing from the file. The only way she knew that the document was missing from the file handed to her by the CBA is that Morris had given her a file that contained her original investment instructions. She said that the missing file 'was the original one where I set up with Don Nguyen on the first day in 2002 that I was conservative and that I would always only use proceeds from capital and that was missing'. The committee that heard the evidence of victims of the bank ended up recommending that there should be a royal commission to probe these issues further.

MORRIS ON THE CORPORATE REGULATOR

ASIC's performance was a great disappointment to Morris. The lack of regulatory enthusiasm meant that the bank was able to do everything possible in the short to medium term to try and clean up the optics of their situation and the fact that three whistle blowers were prepared to provide specific intelligence that would assist did not appear to get them to move with any great speed. 'It is a business where even ASIC said there were fundamental widespread problems with the advice. Of the 7,000 pieces of advice that were reviewed, 16 per cent of them resulted in compensation being paid. That is a massive proportion. It is a business that was clearly non-compliant,' Morris said. 'To say there were only seven rogue planners and only 7,000 pieces of advice that needed to be considered in that environment I think is ludicrous. I suspect a broader review is going to uncover there are a lot more, like tens of thousands of clients, who are probably entitled to compensation. It has never been looked at.'

HUMAN COSTS OF WHISTLE BLOWING

Morris warned his two comrades in arms in the whistle blowing exercise that there would be a cost to them and that it is unlikely they would survive the aftermath. One of the whistle blowers left the bank at the end of June 2009, Morris noted in his written submission, and this was the colleague that was given the going over by the bank's 'internal cops'. 'In addition to everything else, the interrogation by Group Security had been particularly hard on him.' Despite having walked from the bank, he still went to a meeting with Morris at ASIC to demand they deal with the complaint that had been sent by the three ferrets 16 months prior. Another whistle blower died in June 2010 at the age of 35 having just experienced the joys of fatherhood. He left behind a 16-day-old baby. 'I can't say that the stress I saw him endure caused his death but I am sure it didn't help,' Morris said. 'Ever since his passing I have regretted not acting alone in this matter. I will never know whether it contributed to this premature death.'

THROUGH THE EYES
OF AN ADVOCATE

||||||||||||||||||||||||||||||||||||||||||||||||||

'We see a lot of problems in the car loan market. People buying cars through car dealerships, and sometimes even through brokers who advertise online or through other media and then connect them with the car dealership. Those problems are endemic.'

KAREN COX, FINANCIAL RIGHTS LEGAL CENTRE

'The first issue with credit cards is that people have routinely been given additional credit in circumstances where they couldn't necessarily pay the credit they already had.'

KAREN COX, FINANCIAL RIGHTS LEGAL CENTRE

THE OPENING WITNESS for the Hayne tour de force through the murky swamp of financial services misconduct was a consumer advocate, Karen Cox, from the New South Wales based group called the Financial Rights Legal Centre. Cox is a lawyer by training and hearing the stories of human suffering in financial distress is a common occurrence for her and her colleagues. Cox had horrific stories to tell about the impact of the conduct of financial institutions on those that come to them needing funds to fulfil some kind of life objective. The organisation for which Cox worked at the time she appeared before the royal commission started in 1987 but had a different name. It was known as the Consumer Credit Legal Centre and its original purpose was to ensure that those failing to meet loans they have received from banks or other intermediaries were able to access legal assist to deal with the sharp end of having debt. The Consumer Credit Legal Centre changed to its current name when management reassessed the remit the organisation had developed for itself. Service areas covered by the centre include consumer credit contracts, banking, superannuation and insurance and the centre encountered client problems with each product type on a regular basis. There is also a debt hotline that frequently receives calls from people in strife with 46% of total calls coming from people in the 35-54 age bracket. Folks between the ages of 55-64 make up 16% of callers and 25-34-year-olds make up 21% of calls. The advisory service took 25,000 calls during the 2016-17 period and 17,000 of those calls dealt with credit and debt issues. The remaining 7,000 calls related to insurance matters. It is from these calls that some disturbing examples of inappropriate advice emerge.

Evidence provided by Cox verbally and in her witness statement tells the story of the heartbreak and financial distress caused by financial advisers, brokers and bankers who have failed to fulfil their duty of ensuring that the services they provide comply with the various duties under laws regulating financial advice and provision of credit. Cox and her colleagues see the human carnage that is caused the failure of advisers and bankers to exercise sufficient care when engaging with customers on a regular basis. Bankers and brokers can be tricky and deceptive at times, particularly where a product or products result in a handsome return for the person flogging rather than the individual that may end up being crushed by debt.

TRICKS OF THE BANKER'S TRADE

There are methods bankers and brokers have in their bag of tools to flog specific financial arrangements to clients and amongst those is a flawed practice of using benchmarks to determine whether a particular product may be suitable for a particular individual. Credit providers use benchmarks in the processes of evaluating a customer for a loan, such as the Henderson Poverty Index, and the Household Expenditure Measure, without obtaining specific information from a client. This results in calculations and assumptions that are flawed and that can lead to a transaction that leaves people in financial distress.

The cliché of 'rubbish in, rubbish out' applied to data entry, accounting and statistics equally applies in the context of loan or credit applications. It is problematic when numbers derived from a 'guesstimate' of household expenditure lead to the approval of a loan that a client cannot pay. This was one of many examples aired over the year-long dissection of financial services misconduct during which evidence led naturally to the conclusion that the client's ability to pay off debt was not necessarily the primary concern of the adviser or banker concerned. 'Even where questions are asked about actual expenses, they are rarely detailed enough to prompt a realistic answer, and verification by the lender or broker is rare,' Cox said in her witness statement to the commission. A mortgage broker may say that there is an estimated monthly budget for an average family and ask the client whether the budget represented by the benchmark accurately represents the specific situation faced by a client. The theoretical conversation pursued by the credit provider starts to lose its lustre once life takes a harsher turn and the obligation to pay off the loan begins to bite hard into the income of the unsuspecting client. 'We find consumers are actually very poor at even assessing their own expenditure unless we take them to documents, like their bills and their bank statements to look at what the actual amounts are,' Cox told Orr under questioning during the first day of hearings.

Stories of strange credit outcomes cropped up as people came to the centre seeking legal advice and assistance on debt related matters. These would typically involve advice that is inappropriate and sometimes even show the reversal of a previous decision. Cox told a story of a 72-year-old woman who needed a modest loan for some work around the house. She asked for $30,000, which was refused because the bank decided she was unable to pay the amount back. 'And then inexplicably the loan is granted and it is for $70,000 and it's a bridging loan, and when we inquire with the bank as to why that has occurred, no satisfactory explanation can be provided,' Cox said. Other stories of consumer pain were presented by Cox during evidence including one person who had refinanced debt on a credit card to a home loan. 'We spoke to a fellow just in the last month who had refinanced $100,000 in credit card debt on to his home loan, the home loan had been moved to a second-tier lender, basically, at a higher interest rate,' Cox said. 'So the result of that transaction is that what was a $1,700 repayment is now a $2,800 repayment. And that family is very likely to lose their home, because they simply can't afford it.' Cox observed that there were questions about responsible lending places of some institutions given that somebody had been allowed to accumulate debate of that nature in the first instance.

ISSUES WITH BROKERS

Loans sourced through brokers present their own problems for the people that Cox and her colleagues at the centre see on a regular basis. The list of broker practices that have been of concern to Cox and her colleagues are:

■ The arrangement of larger than required loans to enable the broker to snare larger kickbacks from credit providers.

■ The pushing of customers to sign up for higher cost loans.

■ The selection of credit providers on the lax nature of their own vetting processes.

■ 'Massaging' or even falsifying client details so the consumer gets a loan and the broker gets a commission.

■ Choosing loans from a very limited pool of preferred lenders based on a preferred commission model; and,

■ Signing up co-borrowers who will not really benefit from the loan and have a lot to lose such as their home.

Central to many of these complaints is the existence of a conflicted remuneration model and the pursuit by some brokers of greater remuneration. There are people that have some idea of what they might be able to afford being encouraged by some brokers to consider borrowing more. Cox told Orr and the commission that this would end up with some clients getting a bigger loan and buying a larger property than required. The underlying issues in the circumstances, Cox noted, was the fact that the larger the loan, the bigger the commission for the broker but the greater the hardship for the customer needing to pay the money back. 'The other situation we see is people who are steered into either more expensive loans or loans with more expensive features than they actually require, and sometimes those features are things that we think are actually harmful for the person,' Cox said. 'So a line of credit loan, for instance, is a dangerous and risky product. We see people sold loans where we don't see any reason for why it should have been granted as a line of credit as opposed to a principle interest loan.' Brokers may choose a lender that might have a more perfunctory credit assessment process because the broker believes they may be able to successfully broker that finance deal through that channel. 'At the worst end of the spectrum we see consumers' details being massaged or even completely falsified by brokers. We have also seen isolated cases of out-and-out abuse where often a member of an elderly person's family will deal with the broker to obtain a loan that is secured over an elderly parents' home and the broker may meet the elderly person once briefly, or not at all,' Cox said. And yet they are the main – you know, their home is at risk.

Consumers do not walk away from the situation with a 'clean slate', Cox observed, because there are times when desperation to secure finance leads the broker and client to be complicit with the provision of inaccurate or doctored information to obtain finance. 'In those circumstances where the consumer may be complicit to a greater or lesser extent in the manipulation of their details in order to secure the loan, the broker may use that fact to discourage the consumer from making a complaint, meaning systematic poor conduct on the part of the broker may never come to light,' Cox explained. 'In extreme cases we have seen financial abuse of elders facilitated by brokers who deal exclusively with the abuser even though the elderly person is providing most of the security.'

Cox pointed to statistics from APRA that reveal loans arranged by brokers have a higher risk of default and the interest-only home loans are more likely to be the ones that will lead to default. Cox noted in her witness statement to the commission that 45% of new loans approved by banks in 2015 were interest only loans. She told the commission that brokers were generally subject to similar rules related to responsible lending and that they should not recommend interest-only loans. Cox's organisation has been able to assist people finding themselves victims of irresponsible lending but there was no evidence, according to her witness statement, that lenders monitored broker networks to fix problems with lending practices. Another dodge in the lending game that Cox highlighted was the use of business loans in order to avoid the need to comply with consumer credit rules. These cases posed problems when it came to taking errant brokers or lenders to task as they would require court action as there was no requirement for some of these players to be members of a dispute resolution scheme. 'We have come across licensed brokers who refer people to unlicensed providers when they ascertain the client does not fit mainstream lending criteria,' Cox explained.

CREDIT CARD CRAZINESS

Consumers have been racking up credit card debt and Cox told the royal commission that the Reserve Bank of Australia's statistics published in December 2017 revealed that there were 16.7 million cards in circulation that had outstanding balances totalling $52.9 billion. This was a 24% increase in outstanding balances from the previous year. The helpline at Financial Rights received more calls related to credit card problems than with any other financial product in recent years. Only the 2008-2009 global financial crisis would knock credit cards off their number one ranking. It was during that period that home loan products became the source of greater angst for consumers ringing for help.

There were five major problems with credit cards that kept the team at Financial Rights busy, Cox observed:

1. Credit limit increase offers being given to customers simply because they had a good history of repayment rather than looking at whether they were able to cope with a larger credit limit. This practice declined, according to Cox, once surveillance and enforcement from ASIC began to take hold.

2. The capacity to pay a credit card off being assessed on the basis of minimum payments rather than properly reviewing a client's financial situation.

3. Assessments of additional or subsequent credit card applications by a customer that disregard existing payment obligations and only consider the minimum repayment required.

4. Refinancing of debt that takes place in the context of balance transfer offers but they may not require the closure of the original credit card.

5. High fees charged for credit card usage.

The royal commission heard that automated systems have made the various credit card problems seen by Financial Rights worse. 'We have seen cases where the client has correctly stated their income as a Centrelink payment and correctly stated the amount received but ticked the wrong box by accident, indicating they were receiving that amount weekly rather than fortnightly,' Cox observed. 'These inconsistencies are often not detected by automated processes, although these processes are becoming more sophisticated.' It is unlikely that banks will be complying with their responsible lending obligations, Cox said, if they only looked at information produced by their automated systems because those systems may not have the most current information about a customer's financial situation. Additional credit card issues that have been seen by Financial Rights include consumers that have sought to refinance credit card debt into home loans and consumers that have been bankrupted when a debt collector comes calling. This process can result in the sale of a family home because of the cost of enforcement and trustee fees arising from the involvement of a debt collection agency.

Interest free periods on store credit cards, which are linked to banks or other lenders, cause angst for consumers because some customers are unable to pay the higher rate of interest that applies after the interest free period if money is still owing. There was also the spectre of stores and their staff seeking to encourage customers to buy more on the credit cards so that they use up a credit limit. Sales incentives offered to store staff also placed an emphasis on getting the business through the door rather than concerning themselves about a customer's ability to pay.

CAR YARD CONUNDRUMS

At least one complaint related to car yard finance would be made every few weeks to the Financial Rights helpline. One of the key issues is that there is little or no contact with a lender during the process of arranging a loan via the car dealer. A typical transaction will involve a customer buying a car while also seeking finance for the new set of wheels. The dealer may organise a loan or use a broker to assist the car buyer to get the loan. 'Commissions-based sales create strong incentives for clients to be upsold and for finance to be approved,' Cox said 'This facilitates a range of problematic practices from subtle manipulation of application details, such as suggesting the consumer leave out certain liabilities or state their highest ever earning week for casual employees as their standard week, to blatant fraud, where the broker generates fake details and fabricates documentation to support.' Another problem seen by Financial Rights relates to refinancing of car loans, which results in larger loans for an already depreciating asset. The only result for the consumer ends up being more debt.

A further problem is that consumers may be drawn into buying add-on insurance related to tyres and rims, asset protection insurance and consumer credit insurance. Cox told the commission that many consumers had no idea that they had a product in the first place so they did not raise concerns about it with the centre. 'So we will talk to a lot of consumers where the first they know about the add-on product is where we look into their circumstances, because they're in hardship looking for options for them and go, "What's this premium? Oh, look, you have got consumer credit insurance. Is that something you can claim on?"' Cox said. 'So we're seeing a lot of people who actually don't even realise they have an add-on product which is a concern in itself. Then we see people who know they have got it but felt they had no option but to purchase it.'

The purchase of add on insurance was the obvious result of the commission-driven culture and this also led to people buying insurance products that they were unable to use in the first instance. 'More often than not they are not eligible to claim on the product. So the reasons for that would be because they were unemployed when they got the loan in the first place, because they worked less than the number of hours per week that the product required them to be working in order to be able to make a successful claim,' Cox said. The term used by Financial Rights for the insurance attached to loans and other products is 'junk insurance' because the insurance premiums paid by a consumer will typically be greater than the amount a consumer would get back when a claim is processed.

Add-on insurance, which is offered in various situations, comes bundled with selling tactics that have been a feature of hawking financial products. Cox noted that there were a number of sales tactics used to pester a customer to convince them to buy a product. 'It can be anything from just repeated phone calls, trying to suggest that people need a consumer credit insurance product, that it would be responsible of them to take a consumer credit insurance product; to the types of scenarios we see in car yards where people are literally held for a long period of time in the place where they are signing up for the loan and placed under a lot of pressure; to situations where it's implied people won't get the loan if they don't agree to the product,' Cox observed. Higher charges may be applied to some customers, Cox said, where they refuse to purchase add-on insurance as a part of the transaction. Discounts taken off premiums are also a sales tactic that will involve pressuring people to take advantage of a voucher. 'And when people say they don't want to buy, then there is a big show of saying, "Well you are going to void your $500 voucher",' Cox said. 'People go, "It's $500, I should use my $500 voucher" when in fact it's elusory. It is not an amount they were intending to spend and we would say it is not an amount that is worth spending.'

IMPACT ON CONSUMERS

Consumers that buy dud products under pressure have additional financial pressure placed on them and Cox observed that there are people that have cars repossessed when they most need a vehicle for everyday tasks. 'Sometimes they have disabled kids or other dependents that they need to transport around and buying a car that they can't actually afford and retain means that they then lose that car and they are back into the same position they were of being stuck without transport but with an enormous cost because quite often where cars are repossessed they are sold and there is a significant residual debt which just adds stress,' Cox noted. The team at the legal centre also saw other evidence of hardship or financial difficulty when poor advice or misconduct took place. 'In circumstances where people end up with home loans that they really can't afford in the long term or particularly where they refinance or consolidate debts into their home loan and they ultimately lose the house, that is not only financially costly but heartbreaking for the people involved,' Cox said. 'Some people are single and can actually, you know, look on it as simply money and maybe they can pick up the pieces and start again but for a lot of the people that we talk to, the loss of their home is very closely tied to family memories and aspirations and to their total sense of self-worth.' There are also psychological and physical consequences for people as a result of falling into an ever increasing, spiralling cycle of debt. Poor advice and banker misconduct can lead to individual clients going through stress, relationship difficulties, breakdown of family structures, leads to poor work practices and ultimately an inability of people to make complicated decisions related to their own finances. 'In some cases we see that people either are quite – or exacerbate mental illness as a result of dealing with debt,' Cox observed. Some people threaten suicide. Then there are the ones that take their own life.

MONEY FOR NOTHING

||||||||||||||||||||||||||||||||||||||||||||||||

'AMP strenuously denies the allegation by Counsel Assisting that it is open to find that AMP has committed a criminal offence in providing the Clayton Utz report to ASIC.'
AMP FACT SHEET, PUBLISHED 4 MAY 2018

'The culture and governance practices within AMP revealed by the conduct reflects insufficient concern for adherence to the law.'
COMMISSIONER KENNETH HAYNE

'I consider that AMP may have made false representations to ASIC about the character of the Clayton Utz Report.'
COMMISSIONER KENNETH HAYNE

FINANCIAL SERVICES VETERAN Mike Wilkins stood before the annual general meeting of insurance giant AMP on 10 May 2018 in his capacity as the chairman of the board to tell shareholders that their board was aware AMP needed to change following the public flogging received by the company during the royal commission. Wilkins took over from Catherine Brenner, who departed the chairmanship of the company, soon after evidence related to the charging of fees for no service and the misrepresentations to the corporate regulator received greater public attention. It was a period when directors and senior management appeared to drop like flies in the aftermath of publicity that was given to matters that were already the subject of investigations by the corporate regulator. The appearance of AMP staff before the royal commission, however, amplified the issues and made reputation management a more critical and urgent issue for the financial services behemoth. The AMP brand bled across the pages of the nation's tabloids and broadsheets as stories about board room disputes on how best to deal with the hammering being meted out on the floor at the commission and in the media as a result of the allegations of lying and ripping customers off to the advantage of sales agents. The experienced Wilkins had no choice but to address the very public examination of the company's entrails. 'At AMP, a small number of individuals in our advice business made the decision not to follow policy and inappropriately charged fees where no service was provided,' Wilkins told shareholders that were present for the annual gathering with interested investors. 'The situation was compounded through a series of communications that misrepresented the issue to – and therefore served to mislead – our regulator on several occasions.' Wilkins pointed to the misrepresentations related to activities taking place within its advisory arm. 'Let me be clear. From my perspective, the number of misrepresentations is not what matters. In my view, one misleading statement is one too many. Trust means honesty, even when the news is bad. On both counts, the behaviour was absolutely unacceptable.' A line was being drawn by the company's chairman in a visible, public forum: the conduct was and remained unacceptable. While he outlined other critical aspects of the company's operations and the status of developments, the royal commission and its impact on the company was his headline thrust. The company's share price on 10 May 2018 was $3.96.

The tone of Wilkins' presentation during the 2018 annual presentation was a stark contrast with that of the former chairman, Catherine Brenner, delivered almost precisely a year earlier and under very different market conditions. Brenner's presentation, which was delivered on 11 May 2017 when AMP's share price was $5.20, was her first address as chairman to an annual meeting of shareholders. It would be her last. The company performance was 'disappointing', Brenner said, given that there was some trouble in the insurance side of the business. 'Good performances in most of our businesses were overshadowed by a significant loss in insurance.

Escalating claims volumes saw us take action to reset and stabilise this business,' Brenner said. 'But the reset meant taking a large write-down in our insurance book, which, in turn, led to a net loss at the group level for 2016 of $344 million.' Brenner had no way of knowing at that time that she would be one of several directors and senior management figures to exit AMP – ritual sacrifices on the road to the organisation seeking redemption from shareholders, regulators, financial markets current and potential consumers and the media. Brenner's exit came shortly after that of Craig Meller, the chief executive officer, and Brian Salter, AMP's group general counsel and company secretary. Wilkins assumed the combined roles of chief executive officer and chairman of the AMP board until such a time as a replacement for both roles was found.

What caused the seismic shift within AMP's governance and management ranks? The company was brought before the royal commission as a result of three key areas: how and why AMP charged fees for no service and how that conduct was reported to the corporate regulator. The company's group executive, Anthony Regan, took the stand at the royal commission to give evidence in a case study that would ultimately demonstrate that AMP had a series of rules it developed and enforced internally that were out of step with the law. The rules, according to Commissioner Hayne's interim report, were out of step with 'commercial morality'. The provision of misleading information to the corporate regulator when the company's reporting identified possible breaches of law was the second issue that exercised the minds of the commissioner and counsel assisting. Counsel assisting the royal commission pointed to 20 instances but the financial services giant begged to differ, preferring to focus on type of misrepresentation rather than the number quoted in the interim report by Commissioner Hayne. The third issue of significance was how and why representatives in the top echelon of officers at AMP were involved in preparing a report that would ultimately be handed over to the corporate regulator and presented to the corporate plod as being an independent report.

WHAT WAS BEHIND GETTING MONEY FOR NOTHING?

The issue of fees for no service at AMP in the first instance, arising from a system that AMP applied across its advisory network. There were contractual arrangements that were examined by the royal commission that resulted in clients being charged fees by advice licensees operating within AMP's advice network. There were about 2,800 financial advisers in the network that AMP operated at the time of the royal commission. It was noted in the interim report that a large number of these advisers were authorised representatives of advice licensee organisations falling under the AMP structure. 'So an authorised representative is typically a self-employed adviser as distinct from an employed adviser or representative, and so where someone is directly employed in the employment relationship with the institution, it's not anything other than an employment relationship, whereas in the case of the authorised representatives, they're licensed by the licensee, in our case the ones that you've mentioned predominantly cover the range of authorised representatives, and they typically then have their own businesses, they're self-employed, but it's the case that they will also employ advisers themselves. But those people will also be known as authorised representatives,' said Regan.

These organisations are AMP Financial Planning Pty Ltd, Charter Financial Planning Limited, Hillross Financial Services Limited and iPac Securities Limited. Each of these individual organisations holds an Australian financial services license and is a subsidiary of AMP. Most advisers employed by AMP worked in iPac Securities. It was common for authorised representatives of an AMP licensee to have some kind of ongoing link with clients and this was usually done via a service arrangement. An ongoing service fee would be charged to a client and then given to advisers when the customer buys products issued or approved by an insurance company. Ongoing services provided by an adviser may include but not be limited to calls and meetings between the adviser and the client. It may also include a review of the portfolio a client has with a particular adviser for management. This is a normal occurrence across the financial services sector. Commissioner Hayne and counsel assisting focused specifically on internal policies that were set by management that resulted in the fees being charged in circumstances where clients received no advice. This policy was known as the 'buyer of last resort' and is referred to extensively as the BOLR policy throughout the interim report and other documentation.

The BOLR policy set down rules for advisers that wanted to sell their client book to another adviser. There were also conditions under which the AMP licensee – that is the advisory business – would buy it from the adviser. 'Under the BOLR policy, a book of clients was typically valued on the basis of a four-times multiple of ongoing revenue earned from those clients,' the interim report explained. 'The revenue subject to this four-times multiplier included the advice fees that had been automatically deducted from the client's products in the 12 months preceding the valuation.' AMP would seek to sell a book of clients to another authorised representative and switching off any ongoing fee arrangements while the client remained in the hands of the licensee makes the client book less valuable. Commissioner Hayne said that it was in the financial interests of the licensee to keep the fee arrangements in place so the they could 'recoup the price it had paid for the book'. Clients acquired by AMP as a part of a 'client book' would be designated to the BOLR pool. Regan told counsel assisting at the time of the hearings that AMP was able to provide services to those clients. It lacked the capacity to do so under its previous rules for those clients put into the BOLR pool. Two critical issues were teased out by counsel assisting during the evidence delivered by Regan. AMP did not stop charging or 'dial down' ongoing service fees even though it was incapable of servicing clients sitting in the BOLR pool. There were circumstances in which AMP wanted to stop charging fees but it had not put processes in place to make sure that clients were not charged for no service.

Breaches related to fees for no service were reported to the corporate regulator in January 2009. The breach report lodged with ASIC noted the breach was first noticed by the licensee in September 2008. It was a breach that had occurred a year earlier in September 2007. Reporting the breach to ASIC, however, did not mean that the practice of sucking in money for nothing ended. It was noted in the interim report of the royal commission that there were documents dating back to 2013 and, in some cases, earlier that described a practice of continuing to take money for clients for almost three months once a client was grouped in the BOLR pool. There was also a rule called the '90-day exception' that was developed within AMP in January 2014 following further changes in financial services regulation. Regan told the Commission that this exception could only be granted by the managing director of the relevant licensee within the AMP network of licensed entities. How often was this exception applied? The royal commission's interim report says this was unclear. What is clear is that ASIC was only told on 17 October 2016 that a further practice that still resulted in certain clients paying money for nothing commenced in January 2014.

The interim report also detailed another internal policy called 'ringfencing' that resulted in yet another circumstance in which certain clients could be charged for services they did not receive. Ringfencing involved keeping a book of clients separately from the BOLR pool for later sale to an adviser. There was little clarity about whether those clients that formed a part of a 'ringfenced' cohort were charged fees for a 90 day period as may have occurred in the case of those that were in a BOLR pool but had a 90 day exception applied to them. AMP did not report ringfencing to the corporate cop until 3 May 2017. There appeared to be an inconsistency in accounts regarding the cessation of the ringfencing practice. Regan told the royal commission it ended in November 2016 but other evidence, particularly an email that formed a part of evidence considered for the Clayton Utz report, points to a ringfencing exception being signed off by the head of AMP Financial Planning on 18 January 2017. Regan accepted that his employer AMP had no basis in law to enforce either the ringfencing or 90-day exception.

INTERNAL WHISTLEBLOWING

AMP staff were concerned about the practices that involved the failure to stop charging customers for nothing. Internal emails tendered as evidence to the royal commission pointed to advice being given by AMP's registers and transfers manager that there was a serious risk that AMP would be in breach of its license requirements if clients were receiving no services while still being charged a fee by AMP. There was a series of emails tendered as an exhibit that were sent in June 2015 in which the nature of ring fencing is discussed and concerns about noncompliance with licensing conditions were being raised. 'Maintaining these registers in ring fenced IDs presents several issues for AMP and we are unable to do this for registers. We need to transfer them and dial down the ongoing fees so that we do not breach ASIC requirements,' Susan Wolff, the manager of registers and transfers at AMP Advice, said in an email that was being sent prior to a transfer of a particular register to the BOLR pool. A further part of that email requested that the relevant manager acknowledges that ring fencing registers without stopping the fees being charged to clients for nothing is a breach of the license. It was clear some staff within AMP knew that the practice was a breach of law.

AMP ON THE DEFENSIVE

AMP's 4 May 2018 submission responding to the financial advice round seeked to explain why the 90-day rule and other internal rules were being enforced by the business. The company's submission said that 'mere knowledge of the existence of the 90-day exception should therefore be sufficient to understand that it was illegal' was an over-simplification. Employees that had been provided advice on how the law applied, AMP contended, may be able to conclude that the 90-day exception was a breach of law. The company's submission said that the employees and executives who were not provided legal advice on these issues would not necessarily question the legality of the practice. 'The 90-day exception and ring fencing generally applied in circumstances where there was an expectation that the client register would be on-sold to another Adviser within a reasonable timeframe,' AMP said. Services offered to customers, AMP's submission said, would vary but an annual review of a portfolio is a common feature and it may be understood a new planner or adviser would be in a position to provide it within a short period of time. AMP also pointed to that 'knowledge, or otherwise, of the lawfulness of the 90-day exception, is relevant to individual culpability'. AMP also noted that knowledge that internal rules such as the 90-day exception were a breach of the law is necessary in order to determine if senior management were aware that staff were engaging in unlawful conduct and whether required knowledge exists to prove a breach of the Corporations Act 2001.

MISLEADING STATEMENTS TO THE REGULATOR

It was this set of circumstances that was the subject of a series of representations made over several years by AMP to the corporate regulator, which were during evidence presented at the royal commission found to be misleading. Commissioner Hayne noted that there were 20 occasions submitted by counsel assisting on which the corporate regulator received documents from the financial services company that were misleading. While the AMP's Regan agreed with Hodge the company itself offered a different analysis of the number of misleading statements that were discussed at the royal commission. The

4 May 2018 submission sent by AMP to Commissioner Hayne noted that misleading statements were the subject of a great deal of market interest and that 'it is important to clarify the nature and scope of those communications'. The company did not believe there were 20 misleading statements but admitted that misleading statements were made. '[The] number of separate misrepresentations said to have been made by AMP to ASIC was nonetheless overstated by counsel assisting. The evidence is that there were seven misrepresentations (in 12 communications), not 20,' the company contended. 'These were set out in the report provided to ASIC by AMP in October 2017.' The company said that the report referred to above was attached to Regan's witness statement sent to the royal commission's legal team in March 2018. Commissioner Hayne disputed the company's account and said in his interim report that he saw no reason doubt Regan's evidence 'that between 27 May 2015 and 3 May 2017, the AMP and the AMP Advice Licensees may have made as many as 20 false or misleading statements to ASIC about ongoing service fee conduct'.

THE PRICEWATERHOUSECOOPERS REPORT

One of the pieces of evidence branded as being misleading by Hodge and Regan was AMP's description of the findings of the report done by global accounting firm PricewaterhouseCooopers into its financial advisory practice. AMP wrote a letter to the corporate regulator asserting that the PwC report found no systematic issues. The 86-page report, which was finalised in March 2015, pointed out a series of internal control problems that existed within AMP that needed further work in order to clean up parts of their internal practices. Hodge asked Regan about the global accounting firm's report given that it was AMP itself that referred to the report in a letter to ASIC. Hodge pointed to select highlights throughout the accounting firm's report to illustrate the fact AMP had misrepresented the content of the report to the corporate regulator in correspondence. Hodge referred Regan to the letter in the first two pages of the report that summarise the accounting firm's key findings. One of them was an observation that risk management processes are 'not operating as designed or require updating to ensure that they meet ASIC's expectations and industry better practice'. Several examples of this were offered by the accounting behemoth. 'Examples of these include the three lines of defence framework breach reporting and complaints management processes as well as the techniques that are being used to monitor the adviser network,' the financial advice review sent to the then corporate counsel Salter stated.

Incident reportage was an area that was subjected to review by PwC and one of the matters Hodge chose to highlight to Regan as a further indicator of problems within AMP's system. The report was not full of high praise for AMP's incident reporting mechanisms, 'Incidents at AMP tend to be self-reported or identified serendipitously. The licensees are not taking proactive steps to identify trends and indicators that point to potential breaches,' the report said. 'Furthermore, root-cause analysis of incidents and breaches that are identified is not conducted which means that potential systemic issues are not identified and similar issues are likely to reoccur as rectification is not fed into continuous improvement of processes training and behaviour. Better industry practice incorporates both of these elements into their incident and breach frameworks.' Regan told Hodge that he was not familiar with what the advisory business had done prior to his arrival at AMP but that he was able to say that there was a current program to deal with that aspect of the report. AMP employs a method of internal controls called the three lines of defence model but PwC said that AMP was not implementing that model of risk management properly despite the fact it is one ASIC regards as being critical for good governance in a financial institution. Regan agreed with Hodge that the PwC report into AMP's financial advice arm pointed to systemic issues.

Hodge followed up his inquisition of Regan on the PwC report with further questions related to a letter that was sent to the corporate regulator by Robert Caprioli, AMP group executive – advice and banking, referring to the work done by PwC. The letter from Caprioli made reference to the PwC report and stated that the accounting firm did not find any systemic issues. Hodge pressed Regan further on this matter and he referred to a paragraph from the PwC report that recommended that AMP conduct a 'root cause analysis' to determine whether they are indicative of systemic issues given that a 'root cause analysis'; had not been conducted. It was observed in the report that potential systemic issues remain unidentified and that 'similar issues are likely to reoccur as rectification is not fed into continuous improvement of processes'. AMP's letter to ASIC said that 'we confirm that the audit program has not identified any systemic issues regarding the provision of ongoing services by AMP advisers'. Both Hodge and Regan agreed that the statement made in the letter from AMP about the review of AMP's processes undertaken by PwC was false with the relevant parts of the PwC reports being read during the hearing by Hodge.

THE CLAYTON UTZ REPORT

ASIC investigations into fee for no service practices into AMP and other entities within the financial services sector triggered a call from within AMP for a proper review of practices that related to pooling orphaned clients into the BOLR pool, the 90-day exemption and also the practices surrounding ring fencing. Law firm Clayton Utz was commissioned to investigate the fee for no service saga on 2 June 2017 given that the board of AMP was concerned about the decision of the advice business to implement the 90-day exception rule when some people within the company were aware it was a breach of the law, the recurrence of fees being charged for no service despite the fact it had been an issue of concern for some time and whether the corporate governance and controls in place at AMP were adequate. The board itself was concerned about misrepresentations being made to the board as well as misrepresentations being made to the corporate regulator. While the call for an investigation may seem routine and the reason behind it is clear, interest in this report stemmed not solely from the fact that the board wanted the tyres of the company's financial advice operations kicked by an external party to see what turned up. The greater component of interest in the report from the perspective of counsel assisting the royal commission, which was acknowledged by all sides as being critical of the entity's operations, related to whether the report was in fact independent of management and was it correctly described as being independent when it was sent to the corporate regulator. Was the reference to the report as independent and external to the entity – as some contend – another case of misleading the regulator?

Commissioner Hayne held the view that AMP may have made false representations about the nature of the report on the BOLR matters prepared by Clayton Utz. This view was predicated on a lengthy list of pieces of evidence that began with the fact that AMP received between 22 to 25 versions of a draft report before a final document was presented to the corporate regulator on 16 October 2017. Commissioner Hayne observed that it is more likely that there were 22 drafts supplied by the law firm to the company. There were a series of revisions and deletions made to the report before ASIC released a final official version. Evidence was presented to the royal commission that showed:

■ AMP made recommendations about the content in the drafts either during phone calls or any of the numerous emails that were sent between the company and the law firm. Some of the amendments suggested the removal of the names of senior executives such as Meller, the chief executive officer at the time, and Caprioli, another senior executive at the company.

■ Meller was said to have been interviewed by the law firm in drafts circulated before 21 September 2017. A version of the document said that there were other people involved in the decision making related to BOLR transactions and internal processes for the reporting to ASIC. Meller was in a list attached to the report.

■ A further draft of the report was sent to the company on 24 September 2017 but a similar paragraph referring to additional people that could assist with the investigation did not have Meller's name on it.

■ AMP received a draft on 4 October 2017 and further amendments were made to the report related to whether Caprioli received or didn't receive internal legal advice.

■ Yet another version of the report made its way to AMP on 6 October 2017. This version was the subject of debate and discussion over the previous two days. That report was a signed final report from Clayton Utz.

■ AMP sent an email to Clayton Utz five days later asking for further amendments to the report to be made that accorded with some material provided by Brenner, the chair of the AMP board at the time. One suggested amendment was for the report to observe that Meller had no knowledge of the BOLR processes.

■ Another signed version of the report was sent across to AMP on 16 October 2017.

Commissioner Hayne said that there was a meeting between AMP and ASIC at which the report was presented along with the initial letter of instructions to Clayton Utz. 'Given the sequence set out above, it may be open to find that AMP implicitly or explicitly misled ASIC as to the character of the Clayton Utz report at that meeting,' Commissioner Hayne observed. 'In producing the [report and letter of instructions] to ASIC under a Section 33 notice on 16 October 2017, AMP may have presented to ASIC that the report was "external and independent".'

AMP DISAGREED WITH COUNSEL ASSISTING

AMP addressed issues regarding the Clayton Utz report in its 4 May 2018 submission to the royal commission. It rejected a series of conclusions that were presented as open findings by counsel assisting and argued the report exposed problems within the organisation where the BOLR processes were concerned. 'It was provided to ASIC and must have, by its very nature, been of material assistance to ASIC in progressing its investigation into AMP's conduct. At no point was ASIC required to accept or rely on any of its findings, and was free to, and in fact did, continue with its investigation,' the AMP said. 'It is significant that Counsel Assisting extensively relied upon the veracity of the report in identifying the relevant misrepresentations to ASIC.' The response from AMP also defended the role of various individuals in their review of the report. Brenner's role in the report was described by the AMP as being consistent with good governance. Brenner, AMP contended, sought some clarification of issues. One of those was to address the appearance and non-appearance of Meller in the final document to be presented to the corporate plod. 'Clayton Utz provided a final report to Ms Brenner by email on 6 October 2017. It is reasonable to assume that one of Ms Brenner's key concerns in commissioning the report was to understand the position of Mr Meller, given that he was the then CEO and, prior to 1 January 2014 the advice business had reported in to him. Ms Brenner was no doubt aware that Mr Meller had been interviewed as part of the investigation,' AMP's submission noted. 'It would therefore have been surprising to her to find that the report contained no mention of him. That can be inferred from Ms Brenner's request that Clayton Utz's findings (whatever they may be) regarding Mr Meller be included. Ms Brenner also sought clarification of the use of the term 'senior management', so the report was clear as to who was meant by that term.'

The AMP response, however, stated that board members were surprised at the level of involvement of Salter in the preparation of the report. 'All of the members of the Board were unaware of the extent and the nature of the exchanges between Mr Salter and Mr Mavrakis,' the AMP submission said. While this surprise was expressed in the AMP response, the company defended the report on the basis that there was no evidence to suggest that any changes made by Salter to the report were ones that were disputed by Clayton Utz or that the law firm did not back the report in all of its detail.

Commissioner Hayne reflected on Salter's involvement in the process of amending the Clayton Utz document in the interim report and he observed that AMP contended that people reading the report itself would know that Clayton Utz is the company's legal firm and that – as discussed above – there was no indication Clayton Utz disagreed with anything in the report bearing its signature. 'The conclusion that AMP sought to draw from these two propositions was that AMP had done nothing wrong. Yet, nowhere in its submissions did AMP address what would appear, on its face, to be an unresolved tension between saying, as it did, that the extent of the involvement that the then-Group General Counsel of AMP, Mr Salter, had in preparations of the report was 'surprising'; to the board of AMP, that the board was unaware of the 'extent and the nature of the exchanges between Mr Salter and [Clayton Utz]' and that the 'board had no reason to suspect that the report may not have been prepared in accordance with their instructions; while at the same time impliedly asserting that Mr Salter's numerous interventions in the rafting process were not untoward,' Commissioner Hayne said.

WHAT COMMISSIONER HAYNE CONCLUDED

Evidence given before the royal commission lent itself to the conclusion that their reasons to be concerned about the state of corporate culture at AMP were sound. The conduct described by Regan during his evidence before the commission was seen by the former judge as being symptomatic of cultural problems within the entity. 'As later recorded in relation to the Clayton Utz Report there were senior persons within AMP (I make no finding more precisely that that) who knew of the charging of fees for no service,' Commissioner Hayne observed. 'Internal lawyers warned that this was a breach of law. Despite all of this, AMP provided ASIC with information that was false or misleading.' There were senior managers and staff who knew the extent of the problem. It was also the case junior staff told senior managers about breaches of law. AMP continued with a 'misleading narrative' to ASIC. Commissioner Hayne observed that the conduct revealed cultural and governance issues that 'reflects a persistent and prevalent attitude of senior persons within AMP that it is acceptable to deal with ASIC other than frankly and candidly'. The commissioner also noted that there was possible misconduct related to the preparation of the Clayton Utz report that related to the internal rules that resulted in fees being charged for no service and also the misreporting of that conduct to the corporate regulator. Evidence, Commissioner Hayne observed, existed for there to be every chance AMP made false representations to the corporate plod.

Various individuals were mentioned in media reports on AMP and its operations while the royal commission was hearing evidence from Regan and some of those exited stage left as evidence was being heard or shortly after. These individuals included Brenner, the former chairman of the AMP board, Meller, the former chief executive, and Salter, the former general counsel and company secretary of the AMP. Commissioner Hayne's closing remarks on the case study noted that ASIC had already been looking at entrails that were dumped on the 'table' in the public domain but that there were some people about whom he was unable to offer remarks. 'Having not heard evidence from [Brenner, Meller or Salter], or from any partner of Clayton Utz, I make no findings about their conduct.'

NOTHING NEW TO ASIC

The AMP fee for no service case study ended up getting more publicity in part because of the theatre in which this interrogation occurred but it was not the first time these issues had come before a regulatory authority. AMP's issues were not novel. They had been the subject of inquiry by the corporate regulator over a period of years. They had a much longer history and these factors were highlighted in AMP's own submission to the royal commission and the regulator itself highlighted the longer-term surveillance program it had been conducting over time. It was the corporate regulator that issued some remarks on what was at that time an ongoing investigation to clarify the status of the matter to the extent possible. The regulator is required by law to maintain a high level of confidentiality on individuals or companies being investigated. A statement issued by the corporate regulator noted that the ASIC has been investigating issues involving AMP and its fee for no service practices as discussed during the hearings of the royal commission. 'This investigation has involved the fee for no service conduct and related false or misleading statements to ASIC. ASIC has, as part of its investigation, received many thousands of documents and undertaken 18 examinations of AMP staff. ASIC is also ensuring that compensation is paid to impacted AMP clients,' the regulator noted. ASIC also pointed to the fact that it had been cooperating with the royal commission on various matters that relate to existing and prior investigations. 'More broadly, all financial institutions need to understand the importance of co-operating with the regulator and complying with the law when providing information to ASIC,' the regulator said. 'Making false or misleading statements to ASIC can result in civil and criminal sanctions.'

AND NOW FOR AN INTRODUCTION...

||||||||||||||||||||||||||||||||||||||||||||||||||

'And the whistle blower tells NAB that these people are making up fake payslips, fake ID, fake Medicare cards and the person has seen a little bit of evidence and has also heard from others in the local area market, one of them a branch manager at a different store not involved in the syndicate.'

ROWENA ORR QC, COUNSEL ASSISTING THE ROYAL COMMISSION

'It's a human system, therefore things go wrong. Sometimes things go wrong through dishonesty. Sometimes things go wrong because of neglect, carelessness, or just sheer coincidence.'

COMMISSIONER KENNETH HAYNE

IT TOOK TWO PHONES CALLS. Two phone calls made in September and October 2015 from anonymous individuals to alert the NAB to the fact that something was going wrong across its network of branches in Greater Western Sydney. Allegations of misconduct as well as specific allegations of bribery were at the centre of these calls, which were made some months after the big four bank conducted an assurance review that related to its profitable introducer program. The program, which involved third parties referring possible customers to the bank, already had dark clouds forming above it given that the bank had already looked at some aspects of the introducer program and found that there was a branch that had introducer files and discrepancies in the sale incentives. It took two phone calls for the bank to blow open the entire introducer controversy within its ranks with a full-blown investigation that was to look in forensic detail at all financial arrangements that were finalised as part of the introducer scheme. Accounting firm KPMG was engaged soon after the whistle blower phone calls to take a deep dive into the introducer mess the NAB had gotten itself into. The big four accounting firm had found that one of the big four banks had some serious fraud issues that needed attention and that there was at least $50 million worth of loans that looked problematic.

Misconduct by bankers and other players involved in the introducer program, which was designed to draw customers in like insects to a venus fly trap by using a trusted third party as an introducer or referrer, involved the use of unapproved individuals referring clients of managers; loan approval involving fraudulent or possibly fraudulent documentation; and bankers accepting payments from unapproved individuals. The NAB did report the conduct to the ASIC on 21 December 2015 but early in the new year the extent of the problem the bank had uncovered required it to notify the regulator of a significant breach under company law. The investigation was also expanded and found that the contagion was not confined to Greater Western Sydney. It had spread across the NAB network and cleaning it up required further action than initially thought. The further investigations conducted by the NAB as well as the review conducted by KPMG found the following practices:

■ Signatures were put on consent forms that resulted in payment of commissions to introducers when they were inappropriate.

■ Fraudulent documents were used to facilitate approval of loans.

■ Payments were received from introducers.

■ Conflicts of interest in the form of relationships with introducers were not disclosed.

■ Failures on the part of bankers to meet face to face with customers, and,

■ Acceptance of home loan applications and supporting documentation from introducers rather than the customer.

The NAB told the royal commission at the time of the hearings that there were 60 bankers of interest as a result of investigations with 11,000 loan applications related to those bankers being reviewed by the NAB. That review uncovered 1,132 customers that were considered by the bank to be victims of misconduct. The NAB contacted 617 of the 1,132 customers. These investigations resulted in 10 bankers getting the sack, 10 leaving the bank for other professional pastures and 32 being put through internal disciplinary processes. One of the penalties that hit bankers disciplined by the NAB was a reduction in their incentive payments. How did the program designed to bring new customers to the NAB go so wrong?

INTRODUCER PROGRAM

The program that would become known to Hayne Royal Commission tragics as the introducer program was an incentive-based program whereby people who were third parties to the ultimate transaction received a commission for leads. It was one of two ways for the bank to write business outside of its branch or web-based outlets. The first of the methods was the more traditional, more regulated mortgage broker referral regime. Brokers needed to comply with the relevant credit laws and as such were bound by legislation that has a focus on responsible lending. Introducers were people who were not required to be licensed. They were not required to be bound by responsible lending criteria in the law. Introducers, however, were people who were quite happy to refer people to the NAB to enter into lending arrangements and receive a commission or kick back. There were introducers who dealt directly with the bank while there were other introducers who operated through agencies that provided banks with leads. Those agencies were known as national referral partners and they would aggregate referrals from introducers working for them in exchange for commissions. There were three such organisations referred to in evidence during the royal commission. They were Nexus Partners, Tomorrow Finance and Capital Growth. Folks who were introducers either in their own right or working for a referral partner had the task of spotting potential NAB clients.

It was a program that proved its worth as a lucrative channel for revenue for the NAB but it also proved to be easily exploited by individuals prepared to take short cuts to get business through. The bank managed to get $24 billion in loans between 2013 to 2016 with 8,000 introducers involved in the program at a point in time. The commission paid to those introducers was a percentage of the amount of a loan. Payment of the commission was dependent on the loan application being approved and drawn down. There were some introducers involved in misconduct that received a large amount in commission. The haul in the case of people involved in misconduct hit about $630,000 over a four-year period with one of those errant introducers pocketing $488,000. It was acknowledged by the NAB's former chief executive officer, Andrew Thorburn, during the hearings that the bank had incentives that were inappropriate and the introducer program was a prime example. 'We've had the wrong incentive schemes. You know, we've – take the introducer case. I am sure you are coming to it. That was like... we put the bait right there for people. Right there. Now, they stepped over the line,' Thorburn said. 'That's their own decision. I'm not excusing that. But like we put incentive schemes in place which caused to reinforce and quick repeat cash. Not good.' Thorburn noted in his evidence that the bank was aware the remuneration incentives involved in the introducer scheme caused misconduct and that program was tweaked to try and rid the lucrative program of some of the difficulties. He said that incentive payments should be viewed as rewards for achieving goals rather than an income-generating end in themselves. Thorburn agreed that any remuneration structure that wound up rewarding misconduct was a bad remuneration structure.

TWO MILLION DOLLARS IN HOME LOANS

Evidence was heard during the first round of hearings about the conditions that introducers had to meet. These conditions included a minimum target for both personal or business lending. Documents tendered to the commission stated that an introducer was committed to either $2 million in personal lending or $10 million in business lending. While documents recorded this particular minimum amount, the NAB's Waldron told the royal commission that the amount was not regarded as a 'strict rule' and that the actual amount was never rigorously enforced. 'The reason we have talked about those sorts of levels is because, having an introducer who does one or two loans, we have found that one of the big issues that we have is that they do not understand the process, they do not understand the requirements if they do it once every one to two – first one or two years,' Waldron said. The bank also told its bankers that they needed to maintain the relationship or link with the introducer and the banker that signed the individual up to be an introducer needed to be the contact point. Waldron noted that there was a change to this process at a point in time and 'specific people out in the field' rather than bankers would sign up introducers. 'That doesn't mean bankers don't meet them and so on, but we have a process where we have experts out in the field trying to assess that and make sure that we are meeting all of our requirements,' Waldron said. 'And we also run a process where, if there are multiple referrals coming from one introducer, we attempt to split that so it doesn't just got to one banker.' These changes to the process for signing up and inducting introducers were, Waldron stated, a part of reforms to the program and they included a process for verifying the professional status of introducers. An introducer claiming they were an accountant, for example, would be checked out by a person out on the road to ensure they were actually an accountant.

WHO WAS A CUSTOMER TALKING TO?

Did customers necessarily understand that an introducer was not an employee of a bank? Were the lines blurred? Was it apparent that the referrer was merely an affiliate rather than an employee of sorts with the bank? Commissioner Hayne quizzed the NAB's Waldron on this matter and asked whether Waldron could exclude the notion that people dealing with an introducer would assume they were actually dealing with the NAB in the first instance. 'I don't think I could exclude that, but in remembering that these people that are introducing the loan are well-known to the customer already for some other purpose that the customer knows that referrer for,' Waldron observed. 'So whether it be a solicitor or whether it be a financial planner or accountant or real estate agent, they would have been representing themselves to the customer in that way and for those services. And that is how they would have got to know the customer, through those services.' Further questions were put to Waldron by Orr related to the manner in which introducers were to provide the service of introduction for which they were to be paid a commission. They were centred around the documentation presented as a part of evidence by the NAB as requested by the Hayne legal team. Documentation setting down the rules of conduct for introducers prohibited introducers seeking to refer business associates. 'Referrals should be genuine introductions of third persons unrelated to you. You must not refer yourself or any agent who acts for or on your behalf or any other person that has not come to you through your primary business activities without written approval,' was one of the clauses specifying a prohibition on referring related parties to the NAB for a loan. A further paragraph set down a condition related to serving a customer's need for a financial product rather than the introducer serving their need to earn an income from a commission. 'For example, you must not refer a customer if that customer does not have a genuine need for a referral or the primary reason for that referral is to generate commission, rather than to service the needs of the customer,' the NAB's guide to introducers said. Waldron explained the NAB wanted introducers to focus on the consumer's needs rather than their own. 'The customer is either purchasing a property for some reason. And that purchase would entail a mortgage that is required and, therefore, there is a logical link to a bank,' Waldron said. He agreed following a question from Orr that this customer need that was serviced was remunerated by a commission paid to the introducer.

THE NAB PLACES HEADS ON SPIKES

The calls from whistle blowers in September and October 2015 raised the alarm about conduct within the Greater Western Sydney area that involved significant fraud. Evidence was provided to the commission that the calls involved allegations of a small cartel or syndicate of individuals running a racket that involved bribery for the approval of loans as well as the production of fake documents. The kinds of documents that were falsified, according to the allegations, were payslips, fake identification and fake Medicare cards. There were also $2,800 bribes that were paid by customers for the facilitation of loans. The evidence presented before Commissioner Hayne on these activities reads like a script of a B-grade Hollywood crime flick with these bankers and introducers playing a part in a swindle that would net some of these characters commissions but create problems for the customer that would be faced with a serious debt.

The bank took a series of disciplinary actions including the dismissal of a series of bankers that were found to have been engaging in misconduct following its initial internal investigations. Five bankers were sacked and two introducers had their introducer agreements torn up as a result of the misconduct unearthed by NAB's investigating team. One banker's termination was detailed in an email sent by Fiona Lynch to Katie Carroll on 9 November 2015. 'Hi Katie. Following interview with fraud and admissions from a NAB banker,' the email to Carroll said, 'this employee has been terminated effective today.' The employee attempted to resign. Her resignation was not accepted. She was told she was being sacked by the NAB and that no notice would be paid out to her as a result of the reason for her dismissal. The reasons were outlined in an abridged form in Lynch's note to Caroll. 'You accepted numerous documents in support of lending applications for customers directly from a referral source known as... and that referral source is not a registered introducer with NAB,' the email said. 'Secondly, you accepted identification documents from a person, rather than from the customer directly, also in breach of NAB's policies.' Evidence of bribery surfaced during the investigation into the conduct of this particular employee with the employee accepting payments in cash from a person on 'at least two occasions'. 'On one occasion you accepted this payment before returning it days later,' the email observed. 'You failed to advise senior management of these payments.' This banker sent emails to an individual responsible for the production of fraudulent documents that were critical to getting loans approved by the bank, which was the central criteria to unlocking the rivers of gold that flowed in the form of commissions.

Lynch sent a further email on 1 December 2015 to a broader group of NAB staff about the ongoing progress of what was known as the whistle blower investigation. The 1 December 2015 email told other bank employees that people were summarily dismissed after the two whistle blower calls. Lynch told staff that the disclosures did not name individuals but investigations led to further information that revealed the identity of parties responsible for misconduct. One banker was described as falsely assigning lending application to an introducer that ended up receiving a motza in commissions for doing nothing. The same banker accepted payment to their own personal account from that same individual that received commissions for doing nothing. There were two $1,000 payments, which were paid into the banker's account in July and September 2015 respectively. This banker, identified during the hearing by Orr as the 'first banker' that appears in the 1 December 2015 email, also failed to meet face to face with clients and there was no proper review of documentation.

This meant that fraudulent documents were accepted by default. This banker was the second banker dismissed by the NAB.

A third banker, who was a branch manager dismissed by the NAB, had a lengthy shopping list of misdeeds set out in Lynch's 'whistle blower update'. False allocation of referrals to an introducer with whom the third dismissed banker had a relationship that was not properly disclosed to the bank. 'This banker requested an increase to the commission payment percentage to the introducer with not valid reason to do so. And the contact details provided by the banker was the address of a property owned and occupied by members of the banker's immediate family,' Lynch told NAB staff. 'This banker had a personal relationship with the introducer, which represented a significant conflict of interest and which the banker did not disclose.' The same banker paid $15,000 into a customer's bank account before a customer's loan was drawn down from the bank. This money represented a further conflict of interest for the third sacked banker. 'The banker acted in this manner despite being verbally warned and required to undertake remedial actions following a similar incident in September 2015,' Lynch observed. NAB's own investigation were already familiar with activities of this banker given that the branch at which certain misconduct occurred was the subject of a 'comprehensive assurance review' in April 2015.

Another bank manager took a long walk off a short pier for failing to behave in accordance with the NAB's rules and this case involved this manager accepting documents from an individual that was not a registered introducer with the NAB. Fraudulent documents were received by this branch manager from the fake introducer that were used to secure a loan for a client. Lynch told NAB staff that this manager was 'dishonest in their responses as to the nature of their relationship with the person and the frequency of their communication'. The banker was also aware that the same fake introducer was engaging with other bank employees but they did nothing to stop the practice and no advice was given to bank management about the behaviour. 'This person failed in their role as branch manager to provide appropriate oversight of the lending within a particular branch.

This resulted in numerous loans being supported by fraudulent documentation,' Lynch explained. 'This banker demonstrated a lack of duty of care when reviewing documentation in support of lending applications, which resulted in fraudulent documents being accepted.' Another manager – the fourth dismissal during this period for fraudulent conduct arising from the introducer program – bit the dust.

The contents of a further email, which was sent on 21 December 2015, tendered as part of evidence before the commission, disclosed details of yet another manager, the sixth NAB staff, that was dismissed as a result of the whistle blower investigations. This individual committed fraud by entering false phone numbers in documentation for clients as well as misleading details about referrers. 'You were dishonest in your response when you initially stated you were unaware how identical numbers had come to be entered on different customer profiles, later admitting you had knowingly entered those details,' the email said. 'On multiple occasions you emailed confidential confidence information to your personal email address.' This same bank manager accepted – as did others – documentation from referrers rather than from customers to whom the bank was going to be lending money. Staff working for this manager were instructed by the manager to process applications with fraudulent documents that were provided by an introducer. The same email also mentioned that a whistle blower complaint against another manager was not proven but that a 'review of sample lending files identified some issues, and this was reviewed by Lending Standards Review. Final outcome determined as amber reversible.' 'Amber reversible' is a performance measure that was used inside the NAB and it simply means that there was disciplinary action taken against the manager but they could rehabilitate themselves if they behave better.

TELLING THE REGULATOR

The internal investigations had been done and some heads rolled but nobody bothered to properly tell the corporate regulator about what was happening in relation to misconduct uncovered in specific locations by the NAB's fraud investigators. There was a discussion about matters related to the introducer program during a risk committee meeting in November 2015 and the subsequent meeting in mid-December of the full board of directors. While the board appeared to get some notification of activities designed to eradicate the termites in the timber frame, their story was very different when it came to informing the corporate regulator about what was going on in the bank's introducer program. The regulator was told in a letter that the bank was investigating problems on 21 December 2015 but a full breach report related to breaches of laws of responsible lending was not filed with the regulator until 3 February 2016. The initial letter to ASIC set down certain findings. 'The investigations to date have identified banker fraud as well as potential control breakdowns in the NAB Introducer Program origination and application process and income verification procedures for both personal loans and home loans,' the letter to ASIC from the NAB stated. ASIC was also notified that there were five bankers terminated and that two introducer relationships were terminated.

The time lag between the discovery of misconduct and the formal reporting of a breach to the corporate regulator was cause for animated discussion during the commission's hearing because Section 912D of the Corporations Act 2001 requires the reporting of breaches within 10 days of a 'significant' breach being discovered. ASIC's Regulatory Guide 78 on breach reporting by Australian Financial Services Licensees points to a series of factors that make certain kinds of misconduct significant enough to require a breach report to be lodged with the regulator. Amongst those factors is actual or potential financial loss to clients or the licensee that might be connected with a breach of the law. Two examples that the regulatory guide offers is the giving of inappropriate advice by representatives to clients and also fraud that might take place in the provision of a financial service. Commissioner Hayne questioned the NAB's timing in reporting significant breaches in the interim report of the royal commission, but he was unable to take it much further than to query it. 'ASIC made no submission to the Commission that NAB did not meet its obligations under Section 912D. There is no evidence that ASIC has complained to NAB about the timeliness of NAB's communications about these matters,' Commissioner Hayne said. 'It is to be observed that NAB gave notice under Section 912D by letter dated 3 February 2016 yet had considered it necessary to tell ASIC and the New South Wales Police about these matters five weeks earlier.' Commissioner Hayne said there was no explanation as to how the NAB's conduct in relation to reporting breaches to ASIC could be regarded as consistent with the law's 10-day time limit for breach reporting. The bank argued that Commissioner Hayne 'should not conclude' it breached Section 912D.

THE KPMG REPORT FINDINGS

The KPMG report commissioned into the introducer scheme in December 2015 made its way to the NAB by 15 January 2016 with a series of additional matters the bank needed to pay attention to that included 13 bankers that were identified by KPMG as being persons of interest. There were also eight further introducers that merited further examination. That report, which runs for 22 pages, also points to the potential that someone involved in the introducer program may have been involved in some kind of criminal or organised crime activity. KPMG's forensic work also found a further 11 bankers from the Greater Western Sydney area that merited attention given that they were active during the period the relevant misconduct was taking place. The work done by KPMG was used in concert with existing work done by the NAB to unpick the fraudulent activities and then progress to compensating or remediating customers for the manner in which the NAB's bankers or introducers had treated them.

IMPACT ON CUSTOMERS

Commissioner Hayne heard evidence about the way in which these practices revealed themselves individual transactions with. Waldron's witness statement provided a series of examples of fraudulent and misleading conduct designed to suck commissions from the NAB's till without regard for the impact on either the bank or the consumer. The impact of the misconduct on individual customers was not immediately apparent to the bank, however, because all of the affected customers had one or more things wrong with their application that only surfaced once investigators from the NAB began their deep dive into client files. The investigations involved interviews with customers to better understand the circumstances under which they had obtained the loan and what documents, if any, they provided the introducer to facilitate loan approval.

One case presented before the royal commission, which is outlined in Waldron's witness statement, involved a real estate agent who was an introducer. The customer wanted to discuss the purchase of a property and the real estate agent told the prospective property purchaser that he could help with the process of getting finance from the NAB. This customer was then converted into a lead referred under the NAB's introducer program with the customer handing over supporting documents to the real estate agent. There was also a large sum of money given to the introducer by the customer. It involved $5,000 for an introducer fee, $29,000 for stamp duty and $73,000 to the bank. There was a visit to a branch of the NAB on 15 July 2015 and the customer told the bank during conversations held as part of the investigation process that the introducer spoke more than the customer. The application was processed and system approved on 17 July 2015 while the Approval Application Team completed verifications on 20 July 2015. A valuation was completed on 21 July 2015 and the loan was unconditionally approved the following day. So what went wrong? The customer had five dependents and this information was not disclosed to the bank at the time the loan application was made. 'So in this particular case there's obvious misrepresentation that has occurred between what would appear to be, in here, the banker and the introducer and the customer in terms of what we have been told,' Waldron told the royal commission. 'So we would have been given information, what has turned out to be incorrect information, fraudulent information, around this particular case.' Documentation supplied for this loan application, Waldron noted, would have said there was sufficient incoming income to cover the loan. 'It would have also said there were zero dependents in this particular case. What we – what has happened here is that a discussion has occurred with the introducer, not the customer.' Waldron said that there were also some language difficulties in the case of this customer, but he emphasised that this was no excuse for the failure of the bank to ensure that the right information was supplied.

There were also times customers were not advised of the information that was being submitted on their behalf by introducers paid commission for securing loans. While the previous example related to non-disclosure of details that would have caused the bank to question whether a loan should be approved, some customers had fraudulent documents passed onto the bank without their knowledge that resulted in loans being approved. One NAB customer went into the Lakemba branch on 30 January 2014 in order to get an increase on their current loan with the bank. The banker completed most of the documentation and the customer signed what is known as a 'privacy consent'. The application was processed by the banker and 'system referred'. Amendments were made to rental income and the application was again 'system referred' and there was a further reprocessing of the loan paperwork to bump up living expenses and to reflect the loan the customer already held with the bank. The 'system' then approved the application. Documentation was supplied by the customer to support the application. These documents included payslips and consents. There was no supply of a rental appraisal but a real estate agent provided a rent appraisal on 1 February 2014 and that appraisal was added to the client files at the bank two days later. Internal application approval team members said nothing more was required to satisfy the bank in terms of verification of the customer's financial position. There was an offer sent to the customer on 6 February 2014. There was, however, a minor problem. While the rental appraisal was used in the loan application, the customer had no idea who pulled the rental appraisal together and there was no rental income from the property that was the alleged source of rental income. The property itself was located in a regional area while the real estate agent's office was in a metropolitan city. That rental assessment should not have been relied upon, according to the bank, for the purposes of assessing the customer's ability to pay back the loan. The bank was still investigating this case at the time of the royal commission's hearings.

Compensating customers for misconduct for the difficulty they faced as a result of the activities of introducers and bankers after a fast buck was still an open issue with the NAB during the hearings. The NAB announced a remediation program for clients on 16 November 2017, which was a fortnight before the royal commission into the sector was established, and alerted the market to its outreach. 'NAB has commenced writing to the around 2,300 customers – many of whom live overseas – asking them to participate in a detailed review of their loan, which may include verification of documents submitted at the time of their home loan application,' the bank said. 'Affected customers may be offered compensation as appropriate.' Customers like those outlined above were interviewed by the NAB as part of a wide-ranging review of client files. Commissioner Hayne noted in his interim report that while the conduct occurred between 2013 and 2016 there was no compensation paid to any customer at the time the commission was picking through the entrails of the introducer saga. 'NAB had conducted 11,000 file reviews and had identified as many as 1,360 customers who may have been affected by the conduct,' Commissioner Hayne said. 'But NAB could say only that the amount it expected to pay out was between $9 million and $23 million.' A market briefing by the bank in May 1019 only offered a general assessment of the total remediation provision and no breakdown of how much will be paid to those stung by an introduction.

ASIC'S WHEELS TURN SLOWLY

It was evident that regulatory wheels turn slowly in Australia when you consider the problem of bankers involved in multiple cases of fraud through the NAB's introducer program. The NAB took its own actions against a number of bankers in 2015 that resulted in dismissal from the bank due to misconduct, but it took some years for the corporate regulator to remove some of the financial services professionals from the register of individuals permitted under law to provide financial services and credit advice. Samar Merjan and Danny Merhab were sacked by the bank in November 2015. Both men were permanently banned by ASIC in July 2018. Another former banker, Rabih Awad, was shown the door by the NAB in December 2015 but ASIC banned him from providing financial services and credit advice. He was investigated by the corporate regulator for loan fraud. Matthew Alwan is another banker that was dismissed by the bank in November 2015 but he was only permanently banned by ASIC in October 2018. Each of these bankers was dealt with by the corporate regulator as a result of misconduct that occurred as a result of the introducer program. The bank issued a media release welcoming the bans in each instance.

ENDING THE DUMPSTER FIRE

A decision was made early in 2019 by the NAB to extinguish the chances of another dumpster fire starting as a result of the intro-ducer program. The bank's chief executive, Phillip Chronican, told the world that there would no longer be referral payments to intro-ducers from 1 October 2019. Chronican acknowledged the bank needed to improve, take action and change whatever is required to ensure it became a 'better bank'. 'Through the royal commission we heard clearly that our actions need to meet the expectations of our customers and the community. We need to be simpler and more transparent to earn trust. We have to put customers first, to be a better bank,' Chronican said. 'We want customers to have the confidence to come to NAB because of the products and services we provide – not because a third party received a payment to recommend us.' NAB's chief executive noted the significance of the changes to the banks and the financial services sector but he said that these changes to the introducer program were critical to ensure customers received better outcomes from the bank. 'Like other businesses, we will still welcome referrals and will continue to build strong relationships with business and community partners. However, there will be no "Introducer" payments made,' he said. 'I understand the significance of these changes for our people and our industry, yet I am certain it's the right thing to do. NAB has a significant role to play in leading the change our customers and the community want to see.'

AUSSIE, AUSSIE, AUSSIE

||||||||||||||||||||||||||||||||||||||||||||||||

'Aussie took no active steps towards assessing whether loans other than those that had been identified as affected by fraud or deception might have been affected by some similar deficiency.'
COMMISSIONER KENNETH HAYNE

'The community would rightly consider that Aussie's continued receipt of payments entailed commensurate obligations to inquire whether the brokers had caused harm to borrowers.'
COMMISSIONER KENNETH HAYNE

'ASIC will act against dishonest mortgage brokers who flout the law for their own financial gain with little regard for the interests of their clients.'
PETER KELL, *ASIC* DEPUTY CHAIRMAN

MANAGERS OF FINANCIAL institutions and advisory firms feeling miffed about recommendations in the final report of the royal commission that state they must be forced to report misconduct to a disciplinary board can in part blame the conduct of some mortgage brokers that involved the pursuit commissions and other ongoing payments by lodging of fraudulent documentation in support of loan applications for clients. Some of these brokers were in the throng of mortgage broking specialists that work for Aussie Home Loans, the vehicle that advertised ad nauseum on television with cheery John Symonds plugging the fact that Aussie would save clients' money by finding the best loan option for them. Four Aussie-affiliated mortgage brokers were in the royal commission's cross hairs as Commissioner Hayne and his crew sought to nut out precisely why these four brokers were able to engage in misconduct and, indeed, what role Aussie played in discovering and dealing with the misconduct. The brokers concerned were Shiv Sahay, Emma Khalil, Madhvan Nair and Bernard (Bernie) Meehan. Three of these 'problem children' had their misconduct first reported by the lenders to which Aussie clients were being referred. Aussie uncovered the misconduct involving Bernie Meehan after conducting an audit of Meehan's files that revealed instances of document fraud. What possessed people to commit fraud of this nature? A closer look at aspects of the operations of broking entities is required to get that answer.

These episodes, and other cases of misconduct linked to financial services professional lining their pockets at a client's expense, cast a pall over the broking profession and were amongst the issues that led to the focus on eliminating conflicted remuneration for brokers. A recommendation that neither the Federal Government nor the Federal Opposition would seriously contemplate introducing at the time Australia was waiting on a Federal election to be called. The reluctance to cut a swathe through broker-related conflicted remuneration was understandable, however, because neither major party would want to be seen to be shutting more than 17,000 small businesses down by putting the squeeze on brokers by criminalising such remuneration and financial services laws.

AUSSIE'S OPERATIONS

Aussie had more than 1,000 brokers working within its mortgage broking operation at the time evidence about its operations was being heard at the royal commission. It was subject to a takeover by the CBA and has been a subsidiary of the CBA since August 2017. This also means that Aussie is covered by the corporate governance framework of the bank but the CBA has made no secret of its wish to jettison Aussie since July 2018 given the intense focus of the royal commission and other players in the Australian market on the role of conflicted remuneration in adviser, banker and broker misconduct. Evidence tendered to the royal commission highlighted the commission-based structure under which Aussie and similar entities operate and some of the pressure brokers may feel to meet contractual conditions. Brokers operating within the Aussie structure would receive a part of commissions paid for loans that were successfully authorised with a lender. The remaining part of a commission for facilitating business for a bank would stay with Aussie. Amounts paid to brokers in commission would always be decided on the basis of the size of the loan that was settled with a bank. As a general rule, loans that were for larger amounts would secure a greater commission. There is also another catch in the Aussie operation, according to evidence presented to the inquiry, and that is Aussie brokers had a condition in their contracts that required them to introduce a minimum number of loans. It is plausible that some brokers feeling the pressure to sell to stay within the broking network will engage in misconduct, which ultimately hurts their company and their client. While this may explain the multiple instances of document fraud, it does not justify or condone the underlying unethical conduct in which the brokers engaged. It bears repeating at this point that fraud takes place where people see an incentive to behave badly, seize an opportunity to engage in misconduct and then find a way of rationalising or justifying their conduct. Each of these would be present in cases of document fraud undertaken in the circumstances outlined in the case study featuring the four former Aussie mortgage brokers.

SLACKING OFF ON REFERRALS
TO THE REGULATOR

The broking network did not refer the four errant brokers to their membership body, which has the power to boot the brokers out of the professional network, nor did they refer the brokers to the police when it became clear fraud was involved. This did not occur despite the fact that Aussie insisted that brokers be members of the Mortgage and Finance Association of Australia. Customers engaging with these brokers were left in the dark about the issues underlying the discontinued relationship with specific brokers. This was despite the fact that Aussie was contacted by customers that engaged with one of the brokers that were guilty of misconduct.

SHIV PRAKASH SAHAY

Aussie first became aware of potential fraud conduct by broker Shiv Prakash Sahay in August 2013 when Suncorp called Aussie to talk with the brokering firm's senior manager of lender relationships. This discussion was also followed by a letter that told Aussie the bank had made a decision to strike Sahay off Suncorp's accredited brokers list. Several borrowers had contacted Suncorp about concerns they had regarding Sahay's behaviour as a broker and a series of applications submitted to Suncorp were reviewed. Seven applications for which Sahay was responsible appeared suspect and these were applications for truncations that were submitted between 14 November 2011 and 25 June 2013. Aussie told Suncorp that it would be conducting its own inquiries into Sahay's financial advice to clients. Sahay's contract with Aussie was terminated by the high-profile broking outfit once the risk management team had reviewed the loan applications lodged by Sahay. The termination took place on 9 August 2013 and that same day a series of panel lenders were advised that Sahay and his company, Ask Consultancy Services Pty Ltd, were no longer authorised or accredited by Aussie. Advice was forwarded to panel lenders that they should review all applications filed by Sahay or his company and to take all possible steps to manage applications and loans that were settled by Sahay or his company.

Bankwest contacted Aussie on 17 September 2013 and advised them that it was likely Sahay had submitted false bank statements with applications. Bankwest supplied Aussie with a broker investigation document that detailed their findings on the matter. This paperwork and other material obtained as a result of queries instituted by Aussie would end up being a part of an investigation undertaken by the corporate regulator, ASIC. It was found that Sahay had sought to apply for $7 million worth of loans for 17 broking clients. ASIC issued a media release that said Sahay succeeded in getting approval for loans worth $4.796 million. This resulted in his company receiving $5,500 in commission payments and then ongoing commissions as a result of document fraud perpetrated by Sahay.

Sahay would up pleading guilty to three charges. These charges involved:

■ The making of 13 false statements in loan applications submitted by him to Bankwest and Suncorp on behalf of clients.

■ The making of 23 false documents in support of those false statements, which took the form of bank statements in some cases, and,

■ The use of 26 false documents in loan applications submitted by him on behalf of his clients to Bankwest and Suncorp.

The errant broker was sentenced to 350 hours of community service work for the three charges following the conviction.

EMMA KHALIL

It was an alert from Westpac that pointed to misconduct of a second Aussie affiliated mortgage broker, Emma Khalil, in March 2014. Khalil was also known as Emma Feduniw. Westpac told Aussie that there was a loan that failed to settle on 5 March 2014 because the bank had detected an anomaly with the application. There was a customer that had sought to apply for a credit card at a Westpac branch and the credit card application had income details that were different to those submitted to the bank via Aussie's mortgage broker. The credit card application caused the home loan documents to be reviewed because it pointed to misleading paperwork being filed by the mortgage broker. This revelation from Westpac led to several days of activity within Aussie in order to conduct an audit of the work done by Khalil. The internal investigation was completed within a week of it being requested and showed:

■ 27 of 40 applications submitted by Khalil went to Westpac.

■ 21 of the applications had letters of employment as the only evidence of employment.

■ 11 of the letters accompanying loan applications to Westpac had similarities.

Aussie found that 20 loan applications were sent to Westpac with suspect letters of employment and ASIC later found that Khallil had submitted eight loan applications with fraudulent employment letters to Westpac for loans totalling $2,720,400, with loans ranging in value from $250,000 to $480,000. The corporate regulator charged Khalil with eight offences related to providing documents in the knowledge that they were false and misleading to Westpac.

Five of the eight loans that were the subject of the ASIC charges were approved and these totalled $1,608,400 with Khalil getting a commission worth $6,847.53. Khalil was convicted and fined $8,500 by the court.

MADHVAN NAIR

The third case study from within the Aussie mortgage broking business is Madhvan Nair who was reported to Aussie by ANZ. There were 15 loan applications reviewed by the ANZ and there were five applications that raised suspicions. Those five had an employer owned by the same businesses and also payslips that were identical and they had a $75,000 a year salary package. It was found on closer examination of the documents that most of the people for whom Nair was applying for loans did not work for the employer mentioned in the documentation. There were discussions about Nair's performance as an accredited broker between Aussie and the ANX and both organisations agreed on a course of action related to Nair's conduct. A witness statement from Aussie set down the steps that were agreed between the ANZ and Aussie in the Nair case:

■ Aussie would review Nair's files to determine whether there was consistent fraudulent behaviour across files prepared for lenders other than the ANZ.

■ Nair would continue to be monitored by the ANZ as a 'fraud watch' case with every application sent to the ANZ to be investigated.

■ Aussie and ANZ would meet to consider the findings of Aussie's audit of Nair's records.

■ Nair would be interviewed by representatives of both the ANZ and Aussie.

■ Both ANZ and Aussie would revoke accreditation if it was found that Nair knowingly committed fraud, and,

■ Nair would be given a warning if there was no fraudulent activity found to have taken place.

The ANZ's concerns against Nair were found to have substance by 26 June 2014 and a formal interview with Nair was organised. ANZ had suspended Nair from its accredited list of brokers following Aussie's instructions. Nair was interviewed by the bank on 1 July 2014 and it was decided on 2 July 2014 by Aussie that Nair was to be let go. There was a chain reaction amongst banks such as ANZ, Westpac and St George that terminated Nair's accreditation prior to him being formally struck off Aussie's list of accredited brokers. The accreditation both Nair and his company had with Aussie was terminated by 7 July 2014.

ASIC took action against Nair following investigations into his conduct. The corporate regulator permanently banned Nair from providing credit and financial advice after Nair was convicted on 18 charges that related to home loan fraud. Nair was released after he entered into what ASIC termed a recognizance of $1,000 that came with a condition that he be of good behaviour for three years.

BERNARD MEEHAN

The case of Bernard Meehan was the only one of the four that Aussie itself managed to detect during an audit review of loan applications put forward by Meehan. It was a similar pattern followed by the other three brokers that submitted fraudulent documents with Meehan also submitting payslips, document checklists and loan serviceability forms in the case of nine loan applications to Westpac. Fraudulent activities on the part of Meehan were uncovered by Aussie on 2 February 2015 during file reviews of Meehan's loan applications. Aussie had a rule that it would review the files of brokers who referred or submitted more than 50% of their client loan applications to one company. The underlying logic of such a threshold was that Aussie believed that brokers shovelling that amount of business through to a single bank could be non-compliant in some way or engaging in some kind of fraud. Meehan had sent more than 50% of his customers through to Westpac given that Westpac accepted letters of employment as a valid way of verifying the employment circumstances of possible clients. Concerns were raised by the compliance manager reviewing Meehan's paperwork. It was found that 53% of his loan application submissions went to Westpac and that payslips used to substantiate the loan applications looked similar with the same font and style. Amounts on the payslips were also in whole dollar figures, which was not particularly regular and it was further noted that these payslips were created using MYOB accounting software. The compliance manager kicked the review findings upstairs to a senior compliance manager that pointed to Meehan having committed fraud. Meehan was permanently banned from working in the financial services arena by the corporate regulator.

AUSSIE AND ACTIONS FOLLOWING BROKER TERMINATION

The four brokers disappeared and customers were not told the reason why. Two of Aussie's clients were looked after by Aussie once Sahay had his relationship with the broking firm terminated. Aussie provided them with no detail regarding his termination. Harris told the royal commission that Khalil's customers may be been notified of her termination as an Aussie broker but she was unclear about whether the circumstances were revealed to Khalil's former clientele. There was also a customer that chose to 'lawyer up' when it became clear that their broker, Nair, had engaged in misconduct. The customer was given an ex gratia payment but the rationale behind the payment was not made clear during the hearings. 'Ms Harris was unable to explain the basis for this ex gratia payment, identify the exact sum of the payment, or provide any other details about the payment. After the conclusion of the hearings, Aussie pointed for the first time to a document that it said explained the payment. Why the documents were not produced by Ms Harris, the witness put forward by Aussie to speak about the injury, or were not put to her by those appearing for Aussie during the course of her evidence, was not explained.'

KICKING BROKERS OUT FOR NO SALES

Many of the stories that were told at the royal commissioner related to salespeople, bankers and brokers succumbing to the lure of commissions and bonuses. Attractive hard and soft money commissions feature prominently as a key reason for broker misconduct but that is not the entire story. What happens when a broker accredited with a bank does not meet an arbitrary sales minimum set by the bank? Banks are known to axe brokers that fail to deliver loans to them over a specified period by using their accreditation process. Accreditation is the key that unlocks the door of a bank to a broker and enables them to offer loan products to clients. A broker that does not hold accreditation with a specific bank is unable to offer anything that is a part of the product suite offered by a particular financial institution. The broker must meet performance criteria or face being cut off from being able to recommend bank products to clients. This constrains the ability of a broker to offer a broad range or even the best range of financial products to clients. A point raised by one broker, Mark Harris, is that the threat of accreditation loss could cause misconduct because a broker may deliberately recommend a specific bank's products in order to ensure they are not culled. Harris was flicked by the CBA after it was said he did not generate sufficient business for the CBA over a period of time. Harris is a degree qualified broker and he told the royal commission that he had been involved in mortgage broking for almost 18 years at the time of the royal commission, with his services largely being used by individuals or couples seeking home loans. There were also some business loans he successfully brokered but these were much smaller in number.

Harris set up a broking business with five other brokers called The Home Loan Broker with all of the brokers working as subcontractors to the business, which is the holder of the credit licence each broker needs to do their job. AFG Home Loans is an aggregator and it is through AFG that The Home Loan Broker is able to access various products. Harris occupies a management role within the business and as such he has a low number of loans that he brokers for clients on an annual basis. 'Since setting up The Hone Loan Broker, I have submitted approximately five to six loans a year,' Harris told the royal commission in the first of his two written statements. 'In the 12 months preceding February 2017, I submitted approximately four to six loans. One of those loans was submitted to CBA and was for the amount of approximately $900,000.' Harris noted that he had submitted one loan to CBA in the two years prior to that near-million-dollar transaction and about four other loans to other institutions. He received notification from the CBA on 20 February 2017 that his accreditation had been withdrawn because the bank considered he had not sent enough business its way. 'As part of this ongoing monitoring, we have identified that you have not been active with Commonwealth Bank for some time. Accordingly, we have made the decision to resign your accreditation with the Commonwealth bank in accordance with our agreement with your Head Group, and have advised your Head Group of this decision,' the letter from the CBA said. 'The purpose of this letter is to provide you 14 days' notice, commencing from the date of this notice, that the Bank will exercise its right to revoke your Authority to Act.' The bank also warned Harris that they would not accept any new bank loan referrals from him and that was effective immediately.

OUT OF THE BLUE

Nobody had alerted Harris prior to this letter that there was any level of dissatisfaction with him as a broker. Harris had not received any calls, letters or emails from the CBA that hinted at any dissatisfaction or the withdrawal of his accreditation. He told the royal commission that there was no reference in the letter to his performance as a broker nor was there any alleged or real misconduct given as a reason to flick him off the list. 'I was not aware of CBA or any customer ever being unhappy with the services I provided,' Harris observed. 'Of the loans I had submitted to lenders in the previous five years, I was not aware of any that had gone into arears.' The loss of his accreditation caused him to reflect on what impact any bank removing brokers from their list of accredited individuals might have on broker behaviour. Harris spoke to media about his concerns because the incident highlighted the fact that brokers aware of the threat of accreditation losses might put their own interests ahead of customers. 'I believe that some brokers will feel pressured to sign customers up to CBA loans so that CBA does not revoke the accreditation due to inactivity,' Harris told the commission. In a curious twist to this case, Harris only became aware of an appeal mechanism that was available for brokers that were punted from the accredited broker list as he was getting ready to appear in court to provide the royal commission with his evidence on brokering practices. Nobody, according to Harris, told him.

GAMBLING ON A NEW LIFE IN AUSTRALIA

|||||||||||||||||||||||||||||||||||||||||||||||

'I went into the bank to close my account where my boss came with me to make sure I was closing it because he knew I had a problem. He was trying to help.'

DAVID HARRIS

'Ridiculously large amount of money for somebody who was earning the wage that I do. So I was working six and seven day weeks, pretty much – pretty much the last three years.'

DAVID HARRIS

AUSTRALIA IS A DESTINATION for many people seeking work and a holiday and David Harris was no exception. Harris had all of the typical traits of people coming over from the Old Dart to test their fortunes out on a throw of the dice in the lucky country. He is a roofer and came to Australia on a working holiday visa in January 2013, which was the first time he had moved from the United Kingdom. Harris was 25 at the time and he got a 457 visa so that he would be able to work in Australia. His work involved him in roof tiling and installing plumbing, which earned him an income of $70,000. A pay increase in June 2017 saw him get $77,000. It was a plan for a holiday in 2014 that got caught up in a cycle of credit card debt that saw him turn to his employer to help drag him out of indebtedness as well as learning the hard way that big organisations can be unresponsive when a person confesses to having a gambling problem that required urgent action rather than further temptation through a consistent hard sell for an increase in credit.

Harris' horror ride with credit card debt began when he started to plan to go back home to visit the United Kingdom as well as get dental surgery done in Thailand. He had no credit card prior but was aware that he needed access to enough funds so that his dental surgery could take place while visiting Thailand. His first ever credit card had a credit limit of $10,000 and Harris paid that credit card debt in full when he returned from his overseas jaunt in February 2015. 'I think I put around $6,000 on it for my teeth and a couple of hotel payments, and then I got back to Australia in February of 2015,' Harris said. 'I paid that card off, I believe, within a month and a-half to two months of being back in the country.' It was later that year, Harris told the royal commission, that he had started to use his credit card as a source of funds for gambling. Harris explained he would occasionally gamble but it was usually only with his own money. Gambling on credit never crossed his mind until he had access to the credit card. Harris had begun to gamble beyond his means and this resulted in him using his credit card to make bets. He was transferring cash from his CBA credit card into another of his accounts with the bank as a cash advance. It was only then that he would gamble with that money. 'It was common for me to "max out"; the First CBA Credit Card. That is, I would frequently use the full limit of my credit card, being $10,000. I would then generally try to pay off the balance in repeated chunks. This would sometimes result in full repayment, but would sometimes only result in partial repayment,' Harris said. 'It was common for me to undertake this cycle of maxing out, and then paying off, the First CBA Credit Card. I would usually try to pay down my credit cards, including my First CBA Credit Card, after I won big bets.' This was only going to get worse before it got better.

MULTIPLE CREDIT CARDS

One credit card was apparently insufficient to satiate Harris' appetite for a wager. He succumbed to further promotion by applying for a second credit card in May or June 2015 while his first was still getting 'maxed out'. He was asked to provide paperwork to support the application yet again and the bank approved his application for card number two with a credit limit of $7,000. 'I kept… I kept… I had the… so I think at the time I… I had maxed out the $10,000 card. I was panicking about trying to pay it off, and the only way I could see was to try and win some money to pay it off,' Harris to the commission during evidence. He then applied for a third card. A bank app advised Harris that he could apply for another credit card. That application for a Platinum Awards card with a credit limit of $8,000 was approved late in 2015. This meant Harris was in possession of three credit cards with a combined credit limit of $25,000 and nothing to stop him from gambling that away.

It was around the time Harris got approval and access to a third credit card that offers to increase the credit limit on his first card arrived. He recalled that the CBA sent him a credit increase offer around 26 November 2015. 'The offer came in a letter from CBA, which told me that I was conditionally approved for a credit card limit increase, subject to certain conditions. I accepted CBA's offer. I do not believe that CBA asked me to supply any documents with respect to the credit card limit increase. As a result, the credit limit of my First CBA Credit Card increased from $10,000 to $12,100,' Harris told the royal commission. The credit limit had creeped up to $27,100 and Harris had three cards with which to contend. It was in April 2016 that the bank received a call from Harris because he had a question about depositing cash into his account. A staff member on the service line asked him whether he had considered card consolidation. 'I banked some money at a cash point and it didn't – sometimes it goes – automatically straight into your account, and it hadn't gone in so I rang up the bank to find out why it hadn't gone in,' Harris said during evidence at the royal commission, 'and then the woman started asking why I had three credit cards, saying that they could consolidate into one, so I would – rather than paying the three different lots – rates of interest, they would put it on to my lower rate card so I was paying the lower rate of interest.' Three cards were then merged into one with the same $27,100. Harris had not yet told the CBA that he had serious gambling problems.

ADMITTING TO A PROBLEM

It was in October 2016 that Harris had another discussion with the bank about getting new bank statements in hard copy format because he was unable to print it out from the website. It was at this point that the discussion with Harris turned into another sales pitch. There was an attempt by a CBA staff member to convince Harris that he should increase the credit limit. Harris confessed to his problem. 'The bank proceeded to say that I was eligible for another credit limit increase to which I replied no, and they carried on asking what – what do I want to do with it. So I explained that clearly, I'm a gambler, I have a gambling problem,' Harris said. 'They can clearly see I've got a gambling problem because of the transactions I've been making. I can't understand why they keep offering me more money.' It should have been clear to the CBA at that point that Harris did not want an increase in credit and that he had just called to get a specific statement from them that he was unable to print out from the website.

Harris got a surprise 10 days later. He advised the bank he did not want nor require a credit limit increase but a letter landed in his mailbox advising him that there was a credit increase from $27,100 to $32,000 that was approved by the CBA. How did it happen? Harris increased the credit limits himself by giving in to the black arts of bank marketing that persistently flagged he was eligible for a credit increase. 'I ignored it for around another month-and-a-half or something. And... so at... at that time as well, every time I was making transfers on my bank account, paying my rent or anything, it would come up you are eligible for a credit limit increase, you are eligible for a credit limit increase, every time,' Harris said. The credit limit jumped from $27,100 to $32,000 and then to $35,000. Temptation to this addicted gambler was present every time he logged in to his account and – even though it took a short while – he eventually succumbed.

CUTTING UP THE CARD

Harris' addiction knew no bounds and the card was maxed out again. This caused him to take the drastic step of seeking help from his employer because he knew he was in deep strife. 'I maxed it out within a space of a month, two months, then borrowed $35,000 off my boss to pay it off. I went into the bank to close my account where my boss came with me to make sure I was closing it because he knew I had a problem. He was trying to help,' Harris explained. 'I went into the bank, and they said in the bank that I couldn't close it in the branch. I would have to call up to completely close the account. So I rang the bank to completely close the account, and they said I had to do it in a branch. So ultimately I decided just to cut up the card and not use it for, I think, around three months.' Harris was given the run around by the CBA and the account ended up not being closed because of administrative ping-pong. The card was cut up by Harris in an effort to minimise temptation but it came back again. A request was made for a replacement card. All bets were off once that card arrived because Harris 'maxed it out again in an even shorter period'.

The bank began to chase him for repayments. He was falling behind and there was a constant stream of communication from the CBA attempting to get him to pay the amount owing back. 'I was getting phone calls all the time. A lot of them went unanswered because they were calling from a private number, and I wasn't happy speaking to my bank on a private number and giving them my details when I don't know who is calling me,' Harris said. 'So I lodged a complaint against them because obviously I had reached out to the bank and two – two of the hardest things you can do when you are suffering from any addiction is admit you've got a problem, and reach out for help, and in that phone call with Commonwealth, I tried to do both.' The complaint lodged by Harris disappeared somewhere into the CBA's bureaucratic labyrinth and he heard nothing for several weeks. He did, however, hear on multiple occasions from CBA representatives wanting to remind him that he was up to his eyeballs in debt and he needed to pay amounts owed. This prompted him to initiate a second complaint and this second shot across the bow seemed to cause recalcitrant staff to get a wriggle on. 'I got passed on to the financial assistance team and it probably took three to four weeks of discussions between me and the financial team before we came to an agreement. They offered to knock off the interest, but I basically spelt out in a very long email to them that that wasn't – I didn't think that was sufficient,' Harris explained. 'So they came back with another offer, and they knocked off $10,000 which I agreed to. I started making payments under that agreement, which was $100 minimum a month, but I will try to pay $100 a week. I've been paying my payments and continued to receive letters from the bank saying that I still need to send them through more paperwork for my financial assistance, even though I had already been paying it, and getting more phone calls saying I've missed payments and stuff like that.'

COMMUNICATION INCOMPETENCE

What caused the mess on the CBA's side of the fence in the Harris case? Internal systems within the bank did not record the fact that he had alerted the bank to his gambling problem. It was agreed by the CBA that Harris should not have received offers to upgrade his credit with the bank once he had made clear his wish to cancel the credit card. Somehow the CBA's system kept pushing credit as if it was an illicit drug to somebody that was not in a position to be able to control the impulse that came with persistent gambling. There was no appropriate method of escalating the information within the bank so that his admission to gambling addiction was properly recorded on his customer account. Bank officers also persisted in contacting Harris about information required to process a hardship agreement when he had already contacted, spoken to and agreed to a payment plan with a person at the bank. 'CBA's systems and processes, as they stood at the time of the hearings, were not equipped to adequately deal with people in situations such as Mr Harris's, even when they explicitly sought assistance from the CBA,' the royal commission's interim report said in reference to the Harris case study.

There is a challenge in situations such as dealing with a gambling addict. Gambling is legal, van Horen noted, and at what point should a bank decide to intervene. 'You can quickly see the slippery slope that puts us on if we say you can't spend on gambling. Well, then what about other, you know, addictive spending on shopping or on alcohol or any other causes?' he said. 'So, you know, this is what we've grappled with. Absent any clear legal or regulatory guideline, how do we determine when we intervene and impose limits?'

One of the other challenges faced by the CBA is the internal systems failed to provide information to people selling the idea of credit increases to someone like Harris that there were financial or other problems that had come to the bank's attention. The right hand at the CBA did not necessarily know what the left hand was doing. 'You know, we need to build a flag. There's complexities around all that. But we need to find a way to make sure that if somebody – and you will appreciate there's a lot of people out there – has a conversation that flags a customer could be in difficulty, in the way of other flags for domestic violence, where we then trigger, you know, domestic violence support programs,' van Horen explained. 'We don't have something that triggers a proactive action around a self-disclosed matter like this. And it's something, you know, we want to do something about it, we've got to work out how we can do that, because it's clearly not a simple thing to execute.'

Van Horen told the commission that details of Harris' personal circumstances collected by a person on the bank's customer hotline should have been recorded in some form so that anyone dealing with him was able to see personal information that would then stop people from sending out letters of offer to increase the credit limit. 'We absolutely acknowledge we shouldn't have [sent out other offers to increase the credit limit] – in a perfect world we would have used this information from the telephone call to find its way back into our credit models.'

OTHER CREDIT CARD ISSUES AT THE CBA

The inability of the CBA to properly communicate with clients that had purchased credit card related products or services was not limited to the Harris case study. Stay at home mother, Irene Savidis, found it extremely difficult to get rid of an insurance product that was promoted to her as a part of getting a credit card with the bank. She first applied for a credit card in October 2014 using the online form but was unable to recall whether she selected an option that related to the purchase of insurance along with getting a credit card. Savidis told the royal commission that she was 'conditionally approved' for the credit card and the initial approval related to a credit limit of $4,000. That conditional approval was followed up by Savidis with a visit to a bank branch to tender identity documents to finalise the credit card approval. 'I have been asked whether I attended the Sunshine Plaza branch of CBA on 6 October 2016, and whether I deposited a cheque while I was there,' Savidis said. 'I have no specific recollection of doing this, but if I did so, I believe that I would have done so for reasons unconnected to my credit card application.' It was during her visit to a CBA branch that the hard sell began on credit card insurance.

A staff member at the CBA branch visited by Savidis began the process of hard sell by giving Savidis the impression that taking out insurance with the credit card was prudent. It was put to Savidis that she should get the insurance and that the policy could always be cancelled at a later stage. 'I initially said that I didn't need insurance, but the staff member said a few times that I should get it, and this made me feel like I had to agree,' Savidis said. 'The staff member told me that insurance only cost a small amount per month, like the cost of a cup of coffee, and that if anything happened to me in the future and I had to stop working, the insurance would help me.' Savidis told the CBA staff that she was unemployed at the time she was applying for a credit card. Her best recollection was that the staff member told her that benefits under the policy, which only provided coverage for those that were employed, were still available. Savidis told the royal commission that she felt pressured in taking out insurance. She was also not sure whether she had signed any documents specifically related to credit card insurance nor could she remember being shown a product disclosure statement related to credit card insurance. Savidis did tell the royal commission in her witness statement that there may have been a pamphlet related to credit card insurance sent out by the CBA at the same time they sent her the credit card. A credit card insurance policy, which was run through Comminsure, was activated in October 2014 and a letter confirming this had taken place was sent to Savidis at around the same time.

STRUGGLES WITH CREDIT CARD PAYMENTS

Savidis was struggling to pay the credit card expenses each month and the insurance was also proving to be a burden. Her inability to make these payments caused her to look closely at the bank's website to determine whether there was a way of reducing the cost of insurance. Savidis found information on the website that suggested she was unlikely to get any benefit from the insurance product because she was unemployed and she did not believe she would become terminally ill. 'I tried to cancel the CCP insurance policy several times over the telephone in or around 2015 because I was worried about how much it was costing me and I did not believe that I would receive a benefit under the policy,' Savidis said. A CBA staff member tried to persuade Savidis to maintain the insurance policy but she told the CBA staffer that she was unemployed. 'Eventually, during one of my telephone calls to CBA, I cancelled my CCP insurance policy, I cannot recall the date that this telephone call took place,' Savidis said. She received a letter dated 1 May 2015 that confirmed the insurance policy was discontinued. A policy that only ended up being added in the first place because of the rusted sales culture prevalent at the CBA at that particular time.

THE KINDER SURPRISE FROM HELL

||||||||||||||||||||||||||||||||||||||||||||||||

'Just because the bank has the power to do something does not mean that it is always right to exercise that power.'
COMMISSIONER KENNETH HAYNE

'Because the matter comes to public attention, what the community thinks should be done, or should have been done, may become well known and there may then be public pressure to respond. But that does not mean the relevant standards and expectations did not exist before the public scrutiny of the issue.'
COMMISSIONER KENNETH HAYNE

ONE OF THE KEY AREAS that brought the Coalition's resolve to keep a royal commission at bay undone was the gritty determination of members of the National Party to place banks in a room to explain their conduct and practices including the litany of examples of farmers under financial distress being forced off their land and out of their homes by insolvency practitioners when their loans were in default. There were a series of case studies presented during the hearings and the companies that were lined up in the cross hairs of Commissioner Hayne and the counsel assisting were the CBA, because of their Bankwest acquisition, RaboBank, the NAB and Rural Bank. Misconduct of some description was evident in each of these as it was in one of the case studies that had received an enormous amount of publicity: ANZ and its acquisition of a niche agribusiness loan book from Landmark Financial Services.

The ANZ took over 7,124 farm loans when it acquired Landmark Financial Services in March 2010 but even with its due diligence was ill-prepared to properly deal with the financial distress that famers as a significant group in the Australian economy face when they are in the midst of droughts, floods and seasons that bring in less than plentiful harvests. Australian farmers naturally turn to their banks for an understanding ear and an extension of credit when times are rough, the crops are wiped out or drought makes it difficult to keep stock alive. Commissioner Hayne and his team probed a series of cases in which the bank failed to act compassionately in circumstances that were dire for the individuals involved. There were 13 farming families about which evidence was presented that were the human face of the loan book that was purchased by the ANZ from Landmark. These were not the only families affected and the bank had significant fallout to deal with, debt mediations and complaints to the external dispute resolution scheme. There was also enforcement action taken by the bank against 30 agricultural clients. The ANZ told Commissioner Hayne and his team that there were 34 farm mediations in which it participated between 2015 to 2018. It dealt with a bulk of those mediations in one year with 21 mediations being heard in 2015. A flood of cases went thought the Financial Ombudsman's Service between 2008 and 2017 related to agribusiness clients. There were 41 cases brought to the financial ombudsman in 2014. There were two recommendations from those 162 cases that were adverse to the bank and three adverse determinations. While the statistics regarding complaints to the external dispute resolution scheme may be in the bank's favour, the bank told the royal commission of misconduct and conduct falling below community expectations that resulted in hardship.

Purchase of Landmark by the ANZ ultimately led to farmers to experiencing immense hardship that, according to former senator and farmer, Rod Culleton, saw the financial and physical well being of many people devoted to the land suffer as well as having his own tussles with financiers over debt issues. 'I have come across people with severe mental and physical health issues. This includes people who have attempted self-harm and suicide. I have witnessed this on the frontline around Australia,' Culleton told the Senate in his first speech on 11 October 2016. 'In a meeting at Winton in Queensland with Bob Katter and Alan Jones, I gained an understanding of how many victims the ANZ bank had claimed Australia wide.' How did a bank's management of its farming loan book get to the point where there were people either contemplating or committing suicide in order to disentangle themselves from a darkness in which they found themselves due to debt?

BACK IN THE BEGINNING...

It all began with a vision, a goal, a purpose. The ANZ wanted to establish a greater hold in lending to the agricultural sector and in October 2009 the ANZ board of directors decided to acquire the entity known as Landmark, the royal commission was told by Ben Steinberg, ANZ's head of banking services. This is a quick way to grow a business – just buy one from somebody else rather than wait around for a business segment to sprout shoots and grow organically. It was sold to the board of directors as having a large list of benefits and those benefits were in part increasing profile, according to a strategy document tendered as evidence to the royal commission. 'The proposed purchase and exclusive referral agreement provides ANZ with an opportunity to move ANZ to number 2 in agribusiness and improve commercial market share by almost 1 per cent, enhance our agribusiness portfolio in our targeted industries (cropping, beef, mixed livestock) and geographies (Western Australia, Queensland and New South Wales),' the document said, 'Expand ANZ's rural footprint, customer reach and enrich our farm lending specialist skill base, leverage Landmark network to cross-sell commercial, retail and wealth management products, including maximising retail deposits of existing and future Landmark customers, and providing wealth management products to retiring farmers.' In other words, the underlying purpose was to beef up a presence amongst the national farming community in order to build an agricultural client base the bank hoped would buy more products from other parts of the bank. A further excerpt from that document set out a business model for the referral of business from the Landmark customer base. 'Landmark will exclusively refer customers, with commissions paid by ANZ, at a rate which is lower than the current broker industry norm, referrals and ongoing customer relationships supported by ANZ relationship managers focused on cross-selling the full ANZ product range to currently under-service Landmark Financial Services customers, and the remaining Landmark customer base to be targeted by joint ANZ and Landmark initiatives.' By reading these portions of documents during the hearings Orr sought to ensure that the principle motivation for the acquisition of Landmark was clear. It was about ensuring the bank was able to make money, more money, from the farming sector over time.

The bank was taking a large gamble with an entity that was not regulated in the same manner as a normal bank. Landmark was not a financial institution cut from the same cloth as the ANZ so the same rules that applied to banks did not apply to Landmark. This meant taking some risks in relation to the loan book. A report from McGrath Nicol prepared for the ANZ in preparation for the acquisition pointed to the lack of a similar regulatory framework. This means that Landmark was not obliged to have as stringent a regime in relation to deciding how to lend funds to prospective customers from the farming sector. 'Landmark is not a licensed [deposit taking institution]. As such, is largely unregulated and has limited external pressures relating to the strength of its control environment,' McGrath Nicol observed. 'The LFS regulatory oversight comprises an AFSL requiring Landmark operations to have an external auditor and report on cash liquidity, external auditor and reporting requirements by AWB Limited, lending guidelines and biannual operational review, or audit, and the debentures are required to be sold with a prospectus.' There was nothing requiring Landmark to be tougher than it was in loan evaluation. It also had an incentive scheme for team members that were involved in the writing of business for Landmark. The incentive payments are also mentioned by McGrath Nicol as posing challenges to the regime of approving finance for farmers. The consultant's report into Landmark revealed that financial incentives were a central cause of the poor quality of many of the loans that ended up being hoovered into the ANZ loan portfolio. It was a risk noted by the consultants looking into the transaction and one that was commented on by the internal audit report done by PwC, which revealed that there were issues of policy noncompliance with various client files that were selected for review by the audit team. These issues were flagged by McGrath Nicol in their report on the proposed acquisition.

McGrath Nicol told the bank that the loan book was looking increasingly unhealthy and the bank needed to look carefully at how credit risks were to be managed by the business. 'As the loan book had shown signs of significant deterioration over the past 12 months in respect of both risk rating and security indicators, there was significant risk of managers incorrectly classifying customers by risk rating and/or security indicator which may hide further evidence of deterioration in the loan book portfolio,' the report said. 'Specifically, there may be a large number of loans currently classified in the C1 or C2 risk category which are in fact D1 or D2. Limited credit management resources not being able to closely manage those accounts which require attention as the loan book quality decreases and the number of managed accounts continues to increase.' Evidence was tendered to the royal commission that revealed more information about the decaying state of the loan book once it was in the hands of the ANZ. Landmark's loan book moved across to the ANZ in March 2010 and at that time 433 former Landmark accounts worth $273 million were described as 'high risk or impaired'. The total of impaired or high-risk loans rose from 433 in March 2010 to 1,050 high risk or impaired loans valued at $722 million. Commissioner Hayne noted in his interim report that the latter number made up nearly a third of the loan book that the ANZ had bought into its fold some three years earlier.

BUMPING UP STAFF NUMBERS

The consultants took the trouble to recommend the bank look at bumping up staff numbers to deal with credit management issues that might arise from the acquisition of the Landmark Kinder Surprise from hell. 'ANZ operations may need to consider increasing the number of credit management personnel to focus on the credit risk rating classifications with support from RFMs prior to the transaction being completed or immediately following transaction close,' McGrath Nicol said. 'The objective is to ensure close to 100 per cent of the loans are independently reviewed to assess Landmark's classification by risk rating and security indicator to ensure compliance with ANZ policy, and that problem accounts are identified and a strategy to manage those accounts is put in place.' These concerns about the quality of the business that was being written by Landmark's agents were had for a completely valid reason. It was a reason all too commonly found when Commissioner Hayne and his legal SWAT team pored through documents.

That recommendation from McGrath Nicol for an expansion in resources to deal with rural matters may seem ironic given separate evidence that was submitted to the royal commission about the ANZ's provision of service in the form of physical branches in the rural sector. The bank told the royal commission at the time of the hearings that it operated '10 standalone business centres in rural areas of Australia'. There were 333 rural branches open at the time of the commission's hearings, which is the number of rural branches left over after the bank had shut 91 physical shop fronts over the previous decade. Branch manager and relationship manager numbers in rural areas dropped as well to 541 in 2018, down from the 726 it had servicing farmers and their families in 2008. This trend of a decline in branch manager and relationship manager numbers was presumably not helped by the loss of Landmark staff with agricultural client knowledge during the period immediately following the acquisition of that loan book.

STAFFERS GONE

The ANZ was poorly prepared to deal with the fall out of taking on Landmark customers while also spending time working out the numbers for the provisions that needed to be made for the poor elements of the loan book in the bank's accounts. A significant additional problem for the ANZ was that the bank failed to recognise the need to build a proper industry-specific unit to deal with the former Landmark clients early enough. The failure to establish what was described in the interim report as a specialist agribusiness team meant that there was another serious problem that manifest itself. It also meant that there was no real expertise within the ANZ itself when staff that worked for Landmark began to leave the ANZ. While the bank had sought to keep almost 80% of the staff, 10% of those landmark staffers left within six months of joining the ANZ. Other Landmark staff members left shortly afterwards. The customers might still have been with the bank but the staff that understood the sector and had dealt with the clients over a longer-term period walked. Corporate memory vanished. People who knew what they were doing were leaving. This could only result in poor outcomes for both the organisation and its clients in specific circumstances over time.

EXPLAINING THE BANK'S CONDUCT TOWARDS FARMERS

The ANZ was aware that the state of the Landmark loan book was poor. Commissioner Hayne noted that it can be inferred from evidence presented during the hearings that assumptions were made in analysing the acquisition. Board minutes of a meeting of the board of directors of the ANZ in October 2016 observed that 'there is a lesson to be learned from the Landmark acquisition in connection with the assumptions that were made around delinquencies that were not stress tested'. This observation made in October 2016 about an acquisition planned for in September-October 2009 and then given effect to in March 2010 may be charitably described as taking full advantage of the benefits of hindsight. Steinberg had told the royal commission the he was not aware of the numbers being stress tested. A failure to more thoroughly crunch the loan book numbers was not the only issue that created a problem. ANZ did not develop a proper agribusiness lending unit until August 2014 and there were customers that did not get a face to face meeting with a banker for more than two years. In other words, there was an absence of 'care and maintenance' of the relationship with the client. Greater stress was also placed on farmers by the bank when there was a refusal to provide funding for the planting of crops or there were demands made for payment of loan interest when it was most likely to send the farmers spiralling further into a financial abyss. Use of law firms was a habit for ANZ's lending services team when it came to dealing with customers in financial strife before they established their specialist agribusiness unit in August 2014. While the bank was using the mechanism of administration under insolvency laws to bring loan default issues to a head, it has subsequently acknowledged that various cases could have been more compassionately handled. Steinberg told the royal commission that the bank sometimes got the consent from customers to appoint an administrator but there were instances where the wind-up specialists were called in without the customer's approval. 'So there might be instances where there has been an insolvency, so a liquidation of a company or a bankruptcy of an individual. Outside of that, at the moment it's – it's fairly rare,' Steinberg told the commission during his stint in the witness box. Fewer enforcement actions have taken place since 2014 as a result of the bank establishing its agribusiness specialist unit. Steinberg offered the example of only four enforcement actions taking place during 2017 and only three actions up to the time Steinberg presented himself to be interrogated in the Brisbane court room.

THE HARLEY CASE STUDY

The explanations and statements of reflection from Steinberg and others at the ANZ do not alter the personal drama that was faced by customers involved in the case studies presented before the royal commission. Stephen and Janine Harley, for example, were Landmark customers and they ran a sheep farm that was spread across several parcels of land known as the McAllinden Property. The family had been working on the property for several generations and in 2013 – the year in which their financial troubles began to crystalise further – they hit more than a century of working the land. The Harleys had dealt with Landmark since 2004 and financial difficulties had already set in for the sheep farmers at the point at which the ANZ took the Landmark loan book over. Five years of trading losses had begun to wear the family down and they knew some of their land would need to be sold off to meet their debts.

The ANZ bank sent the Harleys an offer in May 2011 to a $2.3 million facility that would expire in February the following year. That facility was accompanied with a $250,000 overdraft. This letter of offer resulted in a mortgage being placed over the property and guarantees given the the family. The family was also required to give further information related to finances. The family fell into arrears in interest payments and failed to provide information requested by the bank. The Harley file was moved to Lending Services and the bank had decided the Harleys needed to sell land in order to reduce the level of indebtedness. Someone at the bank decided to have the land on which the Harley farm stood valued and the Harleys footed the bill for the valuation despite the fact it was ordered by the bank.

March 2012 saw another letter of offer from the bank that put in place a $2.55 million facility that would expire in March the following year. It was expected that the Harleys would repay the debt by March 2013 as a result of selling the land. The Harleys did sell one of the parcels of land in July 2012 and paid down debt. Stephen Harley was struck down by illness and ended up in hospital. Attempts to auction sheep in January 2013 brought no joy and two months later the family subdivided one of their blocks for sale. An auction was held. There were no bids. It was impossible for the Harleys to pay their debts by the end of March 2013. The family ended up dealing with further illness in May 2013 with Stephen Harley having a heart attack. Janine Harley told the bank this had occurred but the bank proceeded to issue them with a notice of default even though it was notified that Stephen Harley was incapacitated due to serious illness.

The bank added to the Harleys stress some months later by making a settlement deed with them in September 2013 that would cause the family to vacate their properties by 1 April 2014, if the debt was not paid by 31 March, give ANZ possession of the land and that the bank could get an immediate judgement for the remaining debt. Steinberg said that such a deed would not be drafted nor would the Harleys be expected to enter into it if similar circumstances had arisen at the time of Steinberg giving evidence to the royal commission.

Commissioner Hayne was critical of the approach taken by the bank given the Harley family situation at the time. One day to vacate the property, the Commissioner argued, was insufficient. 'It is obvious that one day is not sufficient time to vacate a property of the kind in question. It is not to the point to say that the Harleys could have made preparations to vacate the property in the preceding six months,' Commissioner Hayne said. 'Preparations would have required the Harleys to incur costs (in packing their belongings and arranging alternative accommodation), which would have been unnecessary if the debt were repaid before the expiry of the deadline.' Any preparations would have merely added to the stress already suffered by the family as a result of Stephen Harley's heart attack. 'In the circumstances, I find that ANZ's conduct in proffering a deed that gave the Harleys only a day to vacate their property, and provided for immediate judgment if the Harleys did not repay their debt, fell short of what the community would expect,' Commissioner Hayne said. The bank argued its conduct in these circumstances did not fall short of community expectations and it also rejected the notion that it breached the bankers code of conduct.

The Harleys did have some success in selling their land in March 2014. They had gotten rid of five out of nine parcels of land and sold some livestock with the result being the payment of $1.6 million of a $2.5 million debt. A request from the Harleys for an extension of time to sell the rest of the properties was denied in April 2014 and they pushed the Harleys to vacate the properties. This included the property on which the family lived. The bank appointed people to deal with the sale. Steinberg acknowledged that it was likely that the bank would have given the Harleys more time if the circumstances had arisen 'today' to sell the properties. It is important to note that despite acknowledging the Harleys would be treated differently 'today' neither the bank nor Steinberg agree that the banking code of conduct was breached and nor did they accept the bank's behaviour fell somewhat short of what ordinary folks on the street would expect.

The Harleys went through more hassles with the bank following the forced sale of the properties when the bank sent agents in to flog the land off. The price obtained for the land did not cover the remaining debt completely and there was still $309,000 owing with the bank adding $59,000 in costs for the enforcement of the deed. More lawfare ensured between the lawyers for the bank and the Harleys with the bank's legal eagles threatening the Harleys with bankruptcy if they did not pay back the remaining debt by 4 December 2014. Lawyers for the Harleys told the bank's lawyers on 23 December 2014 that the bank could have wiped the debt had properties been sold for a sum that resembled the June 2013 valuations. It was proposed by the Harleys' lawyers that the bank release the family from the remaining debt, but the bank refused. No further action was taken by the bank to recover the remaining funds and Steinberg told the royal commission yet again the bank would have behaved differently and accepted the proposal had the circumstances arisen at the time of the royal commission. Neither the bank nor Steinberg were keen on accepting that the behaviour constituted a breach of the banking code of conduct or failure to meet the ordinary folks' 'sniff test'. The bank eventually gave way and in February 2018 the request from the Harleys for a release from an obligation to pay the remaining debt was granted.

Commissioner Hayne's take on the refusal of the bank to accept the proposal for the elimination of the debt is different to the bank's view. Neither the bank nor Steinberg 'accepted that the ANZ's conduct in refusing the Harleys fell short of community standards and expectations', Commissioner Hayne said. 'I disagree.' The commissioner noted that the bank had required the family to sell all their properties as well as their home during a period of time when Stephen Harley was recovering from a heart attack. A bill for enforcement expenses of nearly $60,000 was added to their obligation and they were without the ability to earn a quid because their farming business had gone. '[The bank] had sold the last four of the Harley's properties in circumstances where those properties had remained unoccupied for several months,' Commissioner Hayne noted. 'It had also sold those properties before the spring, when the Harleys had told the bank there would be the most interest in these properties.' Commissioner Hayne noted that the last two events were precisely the result of the failure of the bank to refuse the family an extension of time to sell properties. The commissioner concluded that this failure to provide more time was neither fair nor reasonable. 'I believe that the community would expect ANZ to have forgiven the Harleys' outstanding debt, as it ultimately did in February 2018.'

The ANZ's lending services arm had been in charge of the Harleys' file for more than 30 months and Commissioner Hayne noted that it was 'impossible to resist the inference "that finalisation" or "completion" of the file had become an end in itself'. While the process to recover funds from the Harleys through what could only have amounted to a liquidation-type sale of remaining land began, the commissioner highlighted another matter related to the management of the Harleys' file by ANZ's lending services team. Nobody – not one person – had bothered to go out to the Harleys' farm and meet with them to discuss their financial issues in person in the two-and-a-half years that lending services had the case in its control. 'Mr Steinberg acknowledged that this was not acceptable,' Commissioner Hayne noted. 'I agree that it was not.'

SENSE OF DÉJÀ VU?

The remarks made by the ANZ regarding the likelihood of treating customers differently when reflecting on the way they treated famers that were deemed to be in default is nothing new. While it appeared novel to those watching the theatrics of the royal commission play out in person or via the webcast, politicians in the Commonwealth Parliament have heard all of this before. A Parliamentary Joint Committee on Corporations and Financial Services inquiry into the impairment of customer loans reported back to the Commonwealth Parliament in May 2016. That committee's report examined the acquisition of the Landmark loan book by the ANZ, which was only one of the entities that was the subject of committee's inquiry, and the ANZ was the subject of a series of submissions that focused on how it dealt with former Landmark customers. Graham Hodges, the deputy group executive officer of the ANZ at the time of the inquiry, appeared before the committee on 13 November 2015 to answer questions about the bank's practices. 'I would like to acknowledge, having reviewed many of the 123 submissions to the inquiry – and, in more detail, the 11 related to ANZ customers, of which five are related to Landmark – that there are some cases where we should have done a better job of working with our customers,' Hodges said. 'As well, there have been examples where we could have done a better job of ensuring that those who act as our agents or who are appointed by us – lawyers, receivers or others – behave in a way that is acceptable to the bank and to our customers.' This was a sentiment that would almost three years later be repeated by Steinberg and by Shayne Elliott, the ANZ's chief executive officer, during the Hayne Royal Commission. Hodges told the parliamentary joint committee in November 2015 that a greater explanation was owed to customers about what the transition from Landmark and the ANZ meant for them. 'A number of former Landmark customers experienced difficulties in operating their accounts during the transition to ANZ in early 2010, but we believe these issues were rectified,' Hodges said. 'Some of these new customers experienced unacceptable delays in our response to both information and funding requirements.' It was noted by Hodges that there were customers grappling with the ravages of drought and that the transfer of the loan book from Landmark to the ANZ made things far more challenging than necessary.

The bank told the parliamentary joint committee in November 2015 – and it would repeat similar words in 2018 before Commissioner Hayne – that changes had been introduced so farmers received more personalised treatment from people who understood that farming sector. 'That is partly because farmers live in their businesses, in a way, so it affects the family and the business, clearly. Key decisions must be elevated to a senior executive for approval. Secondly is ensuring that staff in our specialist team have specific agribusiness experience in managing customers in difficulty,' Hodges told the joint parliamentary committee. 'The staff have greater flexibility to help good farmers manage their way through tough times. Thirdly is improving engagement with agribusiness customers in difficulty by stepping up face-to-face farm visits to understand their individual circumstances.' The very thing the bank told the joint parliamentary committee it was doing in November 2015 – increasing face to face farm visits to understand what farmers were going through – was something Commissioner Hayne pointed to as being absent when the ANZ dealt with the Harley family's circumstances.

QUEENSTOWN – WHAT DO YOU RECKON?

||||||||||||||||||||||||||||||||||||||||||||||

'There was a culture within ClearView Direct that tolerated aggressive sales tactics at the cost of compliance...'
COMMISSIONER KENNETH HAYNE

'Whilst aware of the optics around direct position to budget, this is not a junket or a celebration.'
CLEARVIEW STRATEGIC SALES INCENTIVE PROPOSAL

'We will work with respective departments to reduce tax exposure (FBT implications) and circumvent regulatory barriers (packaged as a training/educational trip in lieu of FOFA/conflicted remuneration).'
CLEARVIEW STRATEGIC SALES INCENTIVE PROPOSAL

BILL CLINTON, the former president of the United States, played golf at Millbrook Resort in Queenstown, a picturesque part of the South Island of New Zealand, in 1999. The Clinton visit brought attention to the idyllic, relaxing environment of Queenstown when he visited the resort, which has a golf course that also hosted a visit by the late Nelson Mandela, a former president of South Africa. Queenstown is also not far from Arrow Town, a part of New Zealand famous for thrill seekers seeking excitement by jumping off a bungee platform. This part of New Zealand is known for its appeal to daredevils and less excitable travellers. There can be no doubt that travel to this part of the world would have been an appealing incentive to sales agents working for insurance company ClearView, who were charged with flogging as much product to customers as they possibly could. It is precisely why one manager within ClearView believed that an incentive program featuring a trip for a limited number of ClearView sales agents to Queenstown, New Zealand, would be of some cultural benefit to the agents. What was of great concern to ClearView heavyweights, however, is that a document tabled as evidence at the Hayne Royal Commission contained an admission that the trip to a fairy tale holiday destination was being framed in a way to mask its true nature as conflicted remuneration. A manager in the direct selling unit at ClearView was the author of the document that brazenly declared that the trip should be characterised as a training or educational event so that there was little chance that it would register as being in breach of financial services legislation. The proposal also looked at the issues of managing tax consequences such as fringe benefits tax liabilities. 'Whilst aware of the optics around direct position to budget, this is not a junket or a celebration. It's a considered investment into the build out of a direct business model for ClearView,' the document said. 'In fact, strategic programs such as this should be seen as a necessary cost of running a direct operation (costs should probably be allocated as a recruitment rather than an entertainment lie item).' The ClearView direct sales executive admitted in the sales pitch to senior management executives that the benefits of a travel-based incentive that included air fares, accommodation and entertainment could not be readily assessed. 'Measuring the return on investment is difficult to quantify. However, we should all be confident with the conceptual notion that the monetary benefits associated with proactively reducing turnover are greater than doing nothing, i.e., simply banking the money,' the rather keen direct sales executive said. The proposal bombed. Senior executives at ClearView were deeply concerned at the implications of running an incentive program that was clearly an example of conflicted remuneration and a breach of the Corporations Act.

ClearView's Greg Martin, the chief actuary and chief risk officer for the insurance business, confirmed to the royal commission under examination by Orr that the incentive did not proceed because it did not represent the culture that the business wanted to put into place. Martin told Orr that he was uneasy about the proposal, particularly because it referred to the notion of 'circumventing' regulation and that this particular proposal was amongst a series of triggers that caused a review of the direct sales business. Martin acknowledged that the proposed Queenstown sales agent junket was not a reflection of a good corporate culture at ClearView. It was designed to reward pushy sellers for writing business – a problem that has been the subject of deep criticism. The proposed Queenstown sales agent junket, which was designed to reward pushy policy sellers, was not the only focus on incentives that were being thrown at staff responsible for sales. Further evidence was presented about the incentive driven culture that included the use of days when staff were encouraged to push towards meeting targets in order to achieve a sales target. There was an email discussed by Martin and Orr that promoted incentives to staff in order to enthuse the sales team to sell 'frenetically' – a word used by Orr – to write business. This added further colour to the previous evidence that had been given by other insurers, bankers and brokers that a significant number of problems arose when overemphasis on selling takes a greater priority than customer needs.

A further matter discussed by Orr and Martin was the nature of the various scripts that sales agents working with ClearView were requested to follow that were designed to lock the customer into buying a product even if they were unsure about the benefits that would flow to them. Sales staff were instructed to ensure they got the customer to sign off on a policy before they let them leave the call.

A tactic used by the sales agents that was revealed in exhibits tendered to the royal commission was to offer to forward the material after the customer signed on the dotted line. One of the scripts was read out in the court room. 'I completely appreciate where you're coming from. I like to think about important decisions as well. Is this because you like to read over everything in black and white? Me too,' the document said. 'The great thing is that I'm going to send out everything to you in black and white for you to read over to make sure everything I've told you makes sense. Putting the cover in place today means you will have the peace of mind that you're covered as soon as you hang up the phone.' Scripts such as these were used by sales agents to pressure customers into agreeing to a sale and then receiving documentation at a later stage. The ultimate, ruthless and commercial objective was to sign people up so a sales agent could get a soft dollar reward, a commission or a bonus for hitting their key performance indicator.

This pressure selling technique was not the only issue the royal commission heard about from ClearView's Martin. ClearView had been engaging with ASIC over a lengthy period of time on matters related to pressure selling. The corporate regulator examined transcripts of calls and the review of 42 sales calls were a primary reason for ASIC to believe that the selling method used by the company could be characterised as 'unfair or manipulative', according to the final report from the Hayne Royal Commission. It was accepted by Martin during evidence that some of the sales calls involved conduct that could be described as being misleading or deceptive and unconscionable. The company was also found by the royal commission to have used opaque language in sales calls that could have resulted in customers not understanding they were buying a policy and payment arrangements were either misrepresented or information was left out during the sales process. Some customers may not have understood how often premiums would be deducted from a bank account, for example. ClearView retained the right to vary premiums and terms of policy application but customers were told that premiums would not go up with age. A further pressure sales tactic was the collection of personal data, such as banking details, before a customer had agreed to purchase a product from ClearView.

UNLOCKING THE MYSTERY OF WHY

What created such a culture where sales targets were given priority over compliance with internal and external rules related to the sale of insurance? The royal commission heard that ClearView's remuneration structure created an incentive for aggressive sales conduct because the more people sold, the more they got paid. There was also a prioritisation of sales targets over compliance, which was epitomised in the case study by the failed proposal for a Queenstown junket for the best writers of business. A further problem faced by ClearView was the fact its internal control function, the quality assurance and compliance program, was inadequate. ASIC reviewed 42 phone calls provided by ClearView. The company's own internal process reviewed 10 of those calls with only a small number of those failing benchmarks. Not everyone at ClearView shared the view of quality assurance team members, however, because the company's own legal eagles reviewed those calls. There was a difference of opinion on the number of calls that were instances of poor behaviour.

Quality assurance is an internal control function and Martin agreed that there was a lack of necessary separation or division between the sales team and the quality assurance team members that would be required to review what the sales team was doing. A greater, more explicit separation between those that were selling and those reviewing the conduct of those in sales could produce a different outcome. Experience in legal and compliance matters was lacking in the direct sales business. This may account for the inability of those selling to better understand where a line was being crossed while a sales agent was on a call trying to convert a reluctant customer into a sale that would deliver a commission or some other reward along the way.

SOURCES FOR REFERRALS

ClearView had two main ways in which it obtained the contact details of potential customers for their insurance products. Martin told the royal commission during the hearings on insurance that the first main source for referrals was its alliance with health insurance giant, Bupa. There was an agreement between the two companies that ensured Bupa would provide a database of customers. 'My understanding is that would typically be a list each month or each quarter. Bupa controlled that list to try and, from their perspective, you know, with their other strategic partners make sure people – their own customers weren't being, you know, pestered, I suppose, if you like, by too many of the strategic partners at the one time,' Martin explained. 'That list was then, as I understand it, either by Bupa or us, washed against or compared to the Do Not Call Register. Customers who were eligible to be called would then be loaded into a – what's called a dialler, or a telephone dialler and that machine would then dial people and assign it to a call agent, I think was the process.' Martin said that there may have been scope for sales agents to select potential customers to call independently of the random dialler process outlined above.

Another way in which targets for ClearView's marketing spiels were provided to sales agents were specific lead generation channels. Some leads may be generated by online competitions where people indicated they were interested in accessing insurance. Other leads may have come from other initiatives put in place by the company. 'Usually they were through some sort of list as well that they would have that would be customers who were – should be suitable. They would inquire of the customers whether they were interested in a call from ClearView. And if they opted in, those customers would then be transferred – I mean the names – telephone numbers and details of those customers would be transferred to ClearView and loaded into a dialler,' Martin explained. The usual process in both of these lead generation processes, the Bupa alliance customer list and other lead channels, was that customers would get sent information by the company and then a call would be made. One element of lead generation for ClearView was also the purchase of contact lists from a series of list brokers. These lists were obtained from companies such as Value Ad, Greater Data Proprietary Limited and Bradford Exchange Limited.

CLEARVIEW AND ANTI-HAWKING

The company's sales agents developed a practice of not giving documentation to customers until after they had agreed to purchase a product, largely sight unseen, but these were not the only sales issues which ClearView had to grapple. ASIC and ClearView had meaningful discussions about the company's tendency to fly by the seat of its pants when it came to anti-hawking provisions in financial services legislations. Concerns at the centre of discussions with the corporate regulator in December 2016 related to the failure to provide product disclosure statements to some customers before they bought a product from ClearView, nor was the product disclosure statement always read to customers. ClearView filed a breach notification with the corporate regulator at some point during December 2016 noting that there was every chance anti-hawking parts of legislation had not been followed for almost two years. More letters between the two parties were sent in order to further clarify that existed within ClearView. The company through Martin admitted that Clearview could have breached the prohibition of hawking products in the Corporations Act 'up to 303,000 times'. These were calls that took place between 2014 and the early part of 2017. How did the company come up with the figure of 303,000 possible breaches? ClearView told ASIC and the royal commission that it was unable to determine whether there was no breach of the anti-hawking rules. There is a degree of nuance and subtlety in this situation that must be teased out. Stating that a company is unable to determine that there were breaches in each of those 303,000 calls just means that the company did not know. Martin told the royal commission that the company did not understand how those provisions worked and as a result it had a large number of possible breaches of the law.

Admitting to possible breaches is one thing but ensuring adequate training and communication on serious breaches is provided is another. Martin responded to evidence that ClearView's internal communication regarding breaches left much to be desired. An email tendered as an exhibit to the royal commission was sent on 14 February 2017 by ClearView's head of group risk and compliance, Simone Leas, with 'Direct business: risk, compliance and cultural issues' in the subject field. The email covered a range of issues but questions put to Martin during the hearing focused on concerns Leas had with culture and oversight. 'The January 2017 direct risk and compliance committee meeting pack did not present the full picture of what occurred with the sales agent who had four anti-hawking breaches in January,' Leas observed. 'All the pack disclosed was "this agent was provided with additional coaching and when behaviour did not improve, she was dismissed". This was a more severe risk and compliance event than was portrayed.' There was a heightened concern within the ClearView business that there were still people within the direct sales division who did not understand what was expected of them as company representatives. Stronger quality assurance was put in place and new scripts were written for direct sales agents but 'following that process that we then discover in ClearView direct that a sales agent is essentially not following the new script, not doing what they're supposed to do, and at that point head office realised that the direct people just didn't seem to be getting it,' Martin said. Commissioner Hayne observed in his final report that Martin was frank in acknowledging that there was something else worthy of consideration in the ClearView context, which is that Martin found it difficult to see how the sales method used by ClearView could both be commercially viable and compliant with the law because there was no way that a customer could get their mind around complex financial issues within the space of the short sales call.

ASIC's concerns ultimately ended up with ClearView agreeing to enter into a remediation program. A media release issued by the corporate regulator on 6 February 2018 announced that the company would be paying about $1.5 million to 16,000 customers. There were 1,166 of these customers that were from indigenous communities. ASIC and ClearView agreed to a series of terms that included the following conditions:

■ Refund full premiums, all bank fees and interest to customers with high initial lapse rates.

■ Refund 50 per cent of premiums and interest to customers with high ongoing lapse rates.

■ Offer a sales call review to other eligible consumers and remediate if there is evidence of poor conduct.

■ Engage an independent expert (EY) to provide independent assurance over the consumer remediation program; and,

■ Cease selling life insurance directly to consumers (that is, without personal financial advice).

Peter Kell, ASIC's deputy chair, said at the time that 'purchasing life insurance is a key financial decision for consumers, and all the information provided to them must be clear and balanced. Insurers should properly supervise their sales staff and ensure that no misconduct is occurring'.

WHAT THE COMPANY TOLD SHAREHOLDERS

ClearView shut down the direct sales business in May 2017 a fact noted in the final report of the royal commission. The company told its shareholders in its financial statements for the financial year ending 30 June 2017 that there were three principle reasons why the company had sought to move out of the direct sales model. Reasons highlighted in the annual report were:

■ Directs sales were failing to make a significant contribution to the company's overall financial health.

■ ClearView was able to focus on its other lines of business such as Advise Life Insurance, Wealth Management and Financial Advice; and,

■ Market attitudes were shifting and telephone sales were not regarded as being economically viable or socially acceptable. Client acquisition costs were increasing, customers were expecting more from the services being offered and there was a likelihood of heightened regulatory scrutiny.

These observations about the closure of the direct sales division were made by the company before the Hayne Royal Commission was called.

A half year report covering the six months up to 21 December 2018 reveals more about the implications of the division's work and the company's own move away from direct selling. ClearView noted in its half year financial statements that it was assessing the final recommendations of the Hayne juggernaut, stating that there was a significant amount of work required within the financial services sector to understand the proposed changes. 'As we work through these and come to more informed conclusions on the potential impacts of the recommendations on our business, we will communicate these as appropriate,' ClearView's half year report said. 'There is no question that the Royal Commission and the other landmark inquiries have been confronting for the entire industry, but ClearView hopes that the reforms will raise the bar on ethical behaviour and accountability in the financial services sector, and repair community issues of mistrust in financial services providers.'

ClearView addressed its appearance before the royal commission directly. The company reminded readers that it shut the direct life insurance business in May 2017 and that it still had the main objective of ensuring remediation payments were made to those affected by the misconduct of sales agents. 'ClearView has implemented the Customer Remediation Program, which covered the categories of consumers and the level of remediation approved by ASIC and final reports on the CRP were provided to ASIC by ClearView and the independent expert on 24 December 2018,' the company noted. 'A further $0.8 million of costs were incurred in the half year under the program. Furthermore, the costs incurred in relation to the Royal Commission were $1.9 million.' The remediation costs were not considered to be a part of the normal course of business for ClearView so they appear below the line in the half year accounts.

THE BAPTIST MINISTER'S SON

||||||||||||||||||||||||||||||||||||||||||||||||||

'We believe that this is unscrupulous conduct at best and that taking advantage of a person with an obvious intellectual disability for the purposes of luring them into buying one of your policies cannot be condoned.'

GRANT STEWART, BAPTIST MINISTER AND FATHER

'Mr Stewart's son was not capable of understanding what he was telling him and he should not have been sold the product.'

CRAIG ORTON, CHIEF OPERATING OFFICER, FREEDOM INSURANCE

'In my view, the conduct of Freedom is to be attributed to its culture and governance practices and its remuneration practices.'

COMMISSIONER KENNETH HAYNE

ONE OF THE MOST egregious and heartbreaking case studies during the royal commission came when Baptist minister Grant Stewart took the witness stand to outline how Freedom Insurance had sold insurance policies to his intellectually disabled son. Stewart lived a life of community service. He had worked as a minister in the

Baptist Church for 35 years at the time of his appearance. A part of his role as a regional minister between 2008 and 2012 involved being responsible for 60 churches across eastern Victoria. Stewart, who is married with three children, returned to serving a parish through ministry in 2012. He told the royal commission he was disturbed when he became aware of how his son was sold insurance by a person from Freedom and 'how little clarifying information Freedom asked for to ascertain whether my son really knew or understood what was being sold'. Stewart told the commission at the time of the hearings that he and his wife were the carers for their son but that he would be moving into community housing. 'My son has some modest literacy and numeracy capabilities and has a degree of independence. For example, he has had his own debit card since the age of 18. However, my wife and I assist him to manage his debit account, and I hold joint authority in respect of that account,' Stewart explained. 'This is because my son has difficulties understanding and managing some financial transactions, including understanding the value of money. For example, my son will usually consult us before buying products. He will often ask us whether he has enough money in his bank account to buy a product and whether particular products are too "expensive".' Stewart told the commission his son needed help to understand the value of different items or products, complex instructions and complex topics. The main source of income for Stewart's son was the disability support pension although he also worked for a couple of hours a week for a family friend for a small payment each fortnight. Freedom's product hawkers sold insurance to his son at a time when his only source of income was the disability support pension.

The royal commission was told that it took some time for the insurance policies sold to his son to be cancelled and Freedom refused to do it without the son's voice on record requesting it despite the father being guardian and one of two carers. Even more bizarre was the fact that it took two years for Stewart to get access to the recordings related to his son's purchase of insurance, which revealed that there was not just the one call but a series of approaches that were made to flog the insurance product to his intellectually disabled son. While the company later apologised for its conduct, the lapse in attention on the part of Freedom's representatives further added to the family's less than stellar experience in dealing with the insurer. Information supplied by Freedom to the royal commission revealed that there were other cases in which insurance was sold to people who were vulnerable.

THE LETTER FROM FREEDOM

Stewart and his wife only discovered their son had bought insurance from Freedom when a letter confirming details of the insurance arrived on or around 14 June 2016. It was unusual, Stewart told the commission, for his son to not have conversations with them about money related matters so the letter dated 8 June 2016, its contents and the fact insurance had been bought was of great concern to the family. 'I read the letter, which said that my son had taken out a Freedom Protection Plan. The letter attached a certificate of membership,' the Baptist minister noted. 'The certificate of membership said that the plan commencement date was 8 June 2016, and that my son had taken out three separate benefits, Accidental Death, Accidental injury, and final expenses – cash back. It was stated in the letter that a premium of $10.60 was payable each fortnight and that the "final expenses" part of the policy had no premium due until the following year.'

Stewart told the commission that he and his wife had never considered insurance of this kind for their son and that he and his wife had their own insurance policies. They made provision for their son in their wills. 'I felt angry that Freedom had signed my son up to the plan,' Stewart said.

It is also usual for packages sent to people that have just bought insurance or another financial product to receive a series of documents. Stewart told the commission that the letter received by his son pointed to other documents being included with the letter. The documents identified in the letter were a product disclosure statement, a financial services guide and brochure. Stewart's witness statement said that he does not remember seeing documents fitting this description when he saw the letter.

CANCELLING THE INSURANCE – FIRST ATTEMPT

The concerned father called the insurance company the next day to try and cancel the insurance his son had bought. Stewart told the commission he highlighted the fact his son had an intellectual disability when a representative from the company told him his son was signed up for insurance during a phone call with a Freedom sales agent. 'The representative said that the sales agent that signed my son up to the plan probably did not know [about the intellectual disability] at the time that the sale was made,' Stewart said. 'I asked to speak with the representative's manager, but the representative told me that she was not available.' An offer was made by the Freedom representative to listen to the phone call during which insurance was sold to Stewart's son and he was told that the insurance could only be cancelled if his son made a specific request for it to be cancelled. The representative had promised to ring Stewart back. 'As a result, I was not able to cancel the insurance during this call. I did not receive a call back from Freedom, as the representative had promised,' Stewart noted. No phone call was forthcoming from the company representative and this spurred Stewart on to write a letter of complaint.

Stewart wrote a letter to Harvey Light, the head of operations for Freedom Insurance, on 15 June 2016 in which he set down his key concerns about the manner in which insurance had been sold to his son. He explained his son's condition to Light and mentioned the receipt of the 8 June 2016 letter that advised his son about the insurance he had been sold by the company. 'It is with considerable dismay that we learned that, as a result we believe of a phone conversation with a member of your sales staff, he had agreed to take out this policy,' Stewart wrote to Light. 'Not only that, but your staff managed to persuade him to give him his debit card details as well.' Light was told that Stewart and his wife believed this to be 'unscrupulous conduct at best' and that 'taking advantage of a person with an obvious intellectual disability for the purposes of luring them into buying one of your policies cannot be condoned'. The letter from Stewart said that the minister hoped that the selling of the insurance policy to his son was an error that would be fixed quickly. Phone calls to the Financial Ombudsman's Service and the Consumer Action Law Centre were also made in order to seek advice on the appropriate course of action. Stewart was advised by the law centre to call Freedom again and ensure his son was on the call with him so that he could give verbal consent for the insurance policy to be cancelled.

CANCELLING THE POLICY

Stewart called Freedom again two days after the first call. His son was on the call on this occasion. A Freedom representative asked Stewart to put his son on the line to have the necessary conversation to get the policy cancelled by Freedom. His son confirmed key identification details to the insurance company's representative and the request for the policy to be cancelled. Their call was transferred to someone at Freedom who would help with the cancellation process. 'The representative spent some time attempting to describe the insurance to us. She told us that my son had taken out a type of cover which was free for the first 12 months,' Stewart said. 'I thought she was telling us this in an attempt to convince us that the plan was worthwhile for my son and that we shouldn't cancel it.' Both men were put on hold while the representative made queries related to the phone call during which the insurance policies were initially sold. The representative of the company returned and said that the company did not believe there were any indications that Stewart's son had an intellectual disability.

A request for copies of the phone calls was met with a request by the freedom staff member for an email requesting copies of the calls. Stewart told the Freedom staff member that he had already sent an email to the company but she told Stewart the email might be considered within two to three working days. Stewart's son was then asked to confirm his full name and date of birth and Stewart asked his son to tell the representative that he wanted to cancel the insurance, which he did. An audit recording of this call was played during the hearing at the royal commission and Stewart told the royal commission that his son 'found it difficult to articulate the words, let alone understand what they meant'. Stewart's witness statement to the royal commission noted that while Stewart was relieved to have cancelled the policies, he expressed annoyance at having to go through a difficult process and the manner in which the company made it tough to exit the policies.

The family felt additional precautions were necessary given the way in which the insurance policies were sold to their son. Cancellation of his son's debit card followed soon after the cancellation of the policy to ensure that Freedom did not deduct funds from the son's debit account. The family also noticed a further effect of the Freedom incident on their son, which was an emerging reluctance to answer incoming phone calls that were from unknown people. 'He became quite apprehensive about answering his phone, and even though we had put his number on the Do Not Call Register, he continued to get phone calls from – we don't know who but he no longer would answer his phone to anyone whose number he didn't know,' Stewart told the royal commission.

A LONG, LONG TWO-YEAR WAIT

A request was made by Stewart for copies of the phone calls that were made to his son in relation to the sale of insurance products. While Freedom Insurance had cancelled the insurance there was no contact with Stewart in relation to the recordings of the calls. The royal commission was told that it was on 8 July 2018 – more than two years after the initial cancellation of the insurance policies – that Stuart approached the company again with a request for all recordings and written correspondence between Freedom and his son and himself relating to the insurance transaction. An authority to disclose was signed by Stewart's son so that as a father Stewart was able to access the material from Freedom. The son's permission for the father to act on his behalf would also avoid unnecessary and administrative delays in getting the information to the Stewart family. A response was received from the company two days later and Ms Delahunty from Freedom said that an internal request has been made for the supply of the material. Stewart sent a further email on the matter. That email sent on 24 July 2018 sought a progress update on the document request. Delahunty did not respond until 1 August 2018 and she said she was hoping to provide Stewart with the documents by 3 August 2018. The response came a day earlier.

Craig Orton was the chief operating officer at Freedom at the time of the hearings conducted by the royal commission. Orton contacted Stewart by email. His email contained as attachments a letter, records of each of the calls and transcripts as well as other relevant documents requested a month earlier. The letter lists 18 separate attachments that record the transactions from the first point of contact with the sales agent through to policy cancellation and also transcripts of five phone calls. Orton's letter notified that family about actions the company took to ensure that the kind of treatment their son received did not occur again. Stewart became aware for the first time that his son received at least three phone calls from the company before he as the young man's guardian and carer learned of the insurance purchase. The relevant phone calls took place on 1 June 2016, 6 June 2016 and then 8 June 2016. 'After listening to these recordings, I felt very disturbed about how the conversation transpired and about how little clarifying information Freedom asked for to ascertain whether my son really knew or understood what was being sold.'

FREEDOM'S RESPONSE TO THE SCENARIO

Orton's letter to Stewart shed greater light on the company's response to the sale of insurance products to somebody a sales agent should have been able to identify as a person that was vulnerable. Orton told Stewart that the sales agent responsible 'exited' the company shortly after the sale because they failed to follow guidelines related to the selling of products to people who were clearly vulnerable. The royal commission was told by Orton during the hearings that he believed the sales agent knew what they were doing when selling the insurance product to Stewart's son. He called the sale inappropriate and also noted that staff had been given training in order to better understand how to deal with vulnerable people. Orton admitted that the company had received further complaints about inappropriate sales to vulnerable customers but that Freedom had introduced focused training for staff on these issues. 'The first vulnerable customer training was put in place in February 2017. It was updated again in December 2017. And then again in March 2018 to make sure that it provided some more practical guidelines on how to deal with vulnerable customers,' Orton told Orr during his evidence. 'And then again in August, there was some more work done and – on how to practically deal with vulnerable customers when you come across them. It's quite a difficult thing to do in some instances, to determine whether someone is vulnerable. In the case of Mr Stewart's son, that should not have been difficult at all.' Specific training on how best to deal with vulnerable customers did not occur prior to February 2017, Orton explained, but the sales agent should never have pressed on with selling insurance to Stewart's son.

DISCIPLINARY ISSUES WITH THE SALES AGENT

The sales agent who sold insurance to Stewart's son was first disciplined almost six months prior to the contentious insurance sale highlighted by the royal commission. There were two written warnings issued to the agent: one written warning was issued in January 2016 and another warning – a final warning – in February 2016. The royal commission heard that the written warnings had no reference made in feedback provided on a fortnightly basis to the sales agent. 'The sales agent's supervisor continued to encourage him to "aim big" and sell more policies,' Hayne's final report said.

REMUNERATION INCENTIVES

The underlying problem leading at least in part to the sale of insurance products by Freedom to vulnerable consumers was the structure of remuneration for sales agents. Freedom used a volume-based remuneration or commission scheme between 2013 to 2015 with tweaks being made to that particular commission model in 2015. The royal commission heard that the company needed to cover the company's cost of having them there to sell product before they could earn commission. In other words, they had to make enough to cover base remuneration and the commission flow would only begin after they had cleared that hurdle. Serious coin would only come later. Freedom called this a 'seat cost'.

'The seat cost was there to encourage them to go to work. That was the main reason [for putting this in place],' Orton said. 'And the other cost was to make sure that it was fair to all of the agents, in that if they were going to utilise better quality leads, that they paid for those better quality leads.'

This lead cost and the 'seat cost' combined into a regime that would only result in commissions in the hands of sales agents once the sales agent covered the costs of them being taken on by Freedom. When it was put to him during the hearings, Orton agreed that this remuneration and incentive structure could lead to aggressive selling. 'I think it can increase the possibility that the salesperson will be pushier, yes, I agree,' Orton said.

There was something else that was revealed during the commission hearings about Freedom's recruitment advertising that focused on the ability of sales agents to get uncapped commissions for selling products successfully. Orton was grilled by Orr on the company's advertising uncapped commissions for product sales, which they were still advertising at the time of the commission's hearings . That regime had been changed by the time Orton fronted to the court room in which the royal commission was being held but the advertising on the company's own website had still been flagging unlimited commissions as a benefit for those employed by Freedom. Orton was unaware that the job advertisements on the website still contained that material. I didn't know that [it was there last week] but yes, it was,' Orton said. 'And that was the website. And I didn't realise it was there. If I had known that was there, it wouldn't have been.'

Freedom also made a series of admissions to ASIC in breach reporting about conflicted remuneration that constituted a breach of provisions of the Corporations Act. One of those acknowledged breaches related to non-monetary remuneration that included travel rewards and what Freedom called 'vehicle incentives'. The company had moved to change its remuneration for representatives so that the various benefits given to sales agents would be within the scope of the Corporations Act. It acknowledged a range of other aspects of its remuneration practices that failed to comply with the law. These were also areas that were subject to criticism from Commissioner Hayne with the chief inquisitor noting that the company's acknowledgements were appropriate in the circumstances.

The company received further criticism in the final report when Commissioner Hayne looked at the areas in which Freedom failed to meet community standards and expectations. There were 27 cases where Freedom engaged in retention and cancellation practices that fell short of expected standards. Retention strategies applied by freedom were also 'heavy-handed' and the company made it difficult for consumers to exit policies they had bought even if they were 'no longer deemed necessary or desirable'. Substandard disciplinary procedures were pointed to in the final report as being a further weakness within the organisation. 'One stark example is Freedom's conduct towards the sales agent who sold the policy to [Stewart's] son: he was encouraged to sell aggressively, even in circumstances where Freedom held serious concerns about his sales practices,' the final report said.

A final area touched on by Commissioner Hayne again referred to the Stewart case study and the failure of the company to recognise the harm its conduct caused Stewart's son. The final report points instance where phone calls were not returned, a request for audio recordings went unfulfilled and a series of disparaging remarks were made about Stewart and his son by internal staff. 'Taken together,' the final report noted, 'these matters indicated a lack of regard for the harm suffered by Mr Stewart's son, and a lack of interest in providing effective or timely redress.'

BED AND BREAKFAST THAT NEVER WAS

||||||||||||||||||||||||||||||||||||||||||||||

'Krish and Karl made us feel like anything was possible and got us excited. We acted on their advice and then they pulled the rug out from under us.'
JACQUELINE MCDOWALL

'As professionals… we should have made it very clear this is not viable. It was poor advice.'
MICHAEL WRIGHT, NATIONAL HEAD, BT FINANCIAL ADVICE

THERE WAS NO EVIDENCE presented to the royal commission suggesting that Jacqueline McDowall and her husband, Hugh, had sought a second opinion when they were planning to retire to a bed and breakfast using a self-managed superannuation fund. This was a significant and life changing transaction for the couple. Jacqueline, a career nurse, and Hugh, a truck driver, were looking to switch gears, adopt a new lifestyle and hoped a new business would set them up for the rest of their lives. Second opinions are the norm when complicated health procedures are being contemplated but they are not always sought when people look at their financial well being and in this case a conversation with a family member, financially aware friends or – even better – a registered tax agent or professional accountant could have saved them a world of woe. The McDowalls had completely trusted and relied on advisers employed by Westpac to provide them with assurance that their plan for a bed and breakfast bought by a self-managed superannuation fund in the first instance were both executable, viable and within the law. This reliance on an adviser and banker at Westpac cost them a family home and shattered their retirement dreams. This was a bullet they could have dodged had they been properly advised that their strategy was not only financially impossible but also didn't comply with superannuation rules.

JACQUELINE'S STORY

The McDowalls' misfortunes with the banking sector began when Jacqueline McDowall contacted Westpac asking to speak with someone regarding a retirement strategy that they had been reflecting on for some time. They approached Westpac in April 2015 as trusting customers, believing that the bank would do the right thing by them as they had banked with the financial institution since their arrival in Australia from Scotland in 2002. 'I spoke to a person who identified herself as Monica Litchfield. I explained to her that I was looking for some professional financial advice about the possibility of using a self-managed superannuation fund to purchase a B&B that Hugh and I could live in and run as a business,' Jacqueline told the royal commission in her witness statement. 'Monika took down my information and later called me back to say that Senior Financial Planner Ramakrishnan Mahadevan would investigate whether what we wanted to do was possible and would get back to me.' Mahadevan – referred to as 'Krish' by McDowall in written evidence and during the examination of McDowall by Orr – was a financial adviser working with the BT Financial Group. He called McDowall back a few days later to get a further explanation of what the couple had planned for their retirement years. 'I remember telling him roughly how much Hugh and I had in our superannuation. I also told him that we had some debts,' MacDowall said. 'I recall Krish commenting that because we had over $200,000 this was enough to go ahead with the strategy. Krish explained he would look into it further and get back to us.'

A meeting was scheduled with Mahadevan on 29 April 2015 at a Westpac branch and it was the point at which the McDowalls outlined the details of their plans for retirement but also details of their personal financial affairs. While the McDowalls had a vision for their retirement and $703,000 worth of personal assets, including their principal residence worth $550,000, they also had a series of debts disclosed to Mahadevan that would need to be factored into any analysis of their plans and whether they could, in fact, pull this bed and breakfast thing off. These debts included a $404,000 mortgage over the house they were living in at the time, an Audit finance debt worth $30,000, a sum of $10,000 owing to Toyota Finance and a $44,000 Westpac Personal Loan. There were also two credit cards the couple had with Westpac that had $11,000 owing.

The couple had approximately $200,000 in combined superannuation that they were looking to move from industry funds into a self-managed superannuation fund. They hoped to use some of that money as security to buy that dream property that would serve as their home and the bed and breakfast business they expected would see them through retirement.

Westpac business banker Karl Sleiman was introduced to the McDowalls by Mahadevan. McDowall told the commission in her witness statement that Sleiman called himself the 'money man' and that she felt he was 'blasé' during the conversation. 'I remember him saying "I am the money man who can help you",' the witness statement said. '[Sleiman] told us he could lend us up to $2 million for a property. He said this without asking us any questions about our finances or looking at any document.' Jacqueline and Hugh McDowall thought $2 million was a bit much. The property they were after would cost them closer to $1 million, or so they hoped.

Mahadevan also raised the issue of insurance with the couple while they were talking about retirement plans. 'Krish said that the insurance we had in our old superannuation funds would be cancelled after the transfer of monies to the SMSF so we would need to take out insurance through the new SMSF. Because the property we were planning to spend around $1 million on, he advised us to take out life insurance for $1 million each to cover the price of the property in the event of death; Flexible Living Benefit insurance of $150,000 each and Total Permanent Disability [at] $100,000 each. As we were planning to purchase a B&B for $1 million, we thought it made sense to take insurance out on this amount.' McDowall said the couple gained reassurance from this and remained convinced that their goal to purchase the property for their retirement plans was attainable. They were told by Mahadevan that it would take at least three months to set the elements of their retirement plans but no longer than five months.

This first meeting was also the one at which Mahadevan recommended the couple sell their principal residence. The McDowalls obtained two valuations of their property because they thought the first at $550,000 was excessive but the second valuation of the property was between $480,000 and $550,000. The house was sold for $485,000 and the funds obtained from the sale were used to pay some of the debts outlined above. Two car loans that the couple had remained unpaid. The McDowalls put their belongings into storage and rented accommodation in different locations across Victoria with the couple ultimately moving to the Northern Territory. It was only later that the couple would come to the painful realisation that the strategy they had sought to put in place was unworkable in more ways than one.

It was not until June 2015 that Mahadevan provided the McDowalls with a statement of advice. That statement of advice contained recommendations that related to the establishment of a self-managed superannuation fund, the roll-over of their balances that were at that time in two separate funds, and the various insurances that were a part of the discussion between the McDowalls and Mahadevan. The couple agreed to put the strategy in place given that they had their desires fixed on a bed and breakfast business, but it became apparent as Orr drilled further that they were not aware of all the costs involved in the advice which they had agreed to implement. The senior counsel assisting spent time taking McDowall through the detail of documentation during the time she was giving evidence. It became clear that the McDowalls were not fully aware of the remuneration that would flow to Mahadevan as a result of the advice that was given to them. There was also the question of a $3,000 ongoing advice payment to ensure that the investment strategy was on track and consistent with what the McDowalls saw as their objectives. This, Jacqueline McDowall noted, was also not properly explained when she was examined by Orr.

OVERRIDING THE PARAPLANNER

It was also revealed during the hearings that Mahadevan had referred the arrangements that the McDowalls had wanted to put in place to a paraplanner, which is a standard process for checking over statements of advice before they are presented to a client. Westpac's Wright told Orr that paraplanning was a part of a series of controls that were introduced into the company in 2014 as a part of a suite of preventative and detective controls. '[Paraplanning] is preventative in the sense that the request for the statement of advice is generated before it's presented to the customer,' Wright said. 'So if the request from the adviser is flawed or there's insufficient information, the paraplanner's job is not just to produce the document; it's to add value in the conversation to make sure it's going to be appropriate for the customer.' Alternative strategies or adjustments to arrangements discussed with clients can be recommended in this process and Orr tendered documents that revealed the paraplanner had identified key issues they felt needed more attention. The first of those was the fee for the ongoing advice service with the paraplanner suggesting that the $3,000 fee was too high and should be reduced down to $2,200 in line with the advisory service category the McDowalls were receiving. Mahadevan said that the fee was appropriate because it was based on the complexity of the advice. This was an amount he would be paid each year for maintaining contact with the couple and reviewing the state of their investment.

It became clear that the paraplanner had documented a series of alternative ways of dealing with the McDowalls' advisory needs that could have had them following a different course and avoiding what ended up being a confrontation with Westpac over poor advice. The paraplanner suggested that the setting up of a self-managed superannuation fund could be delayed until such a time as a suitable property was found to avoid the unnecessary costs that come with establishing and maintaining a self-managed fund if they were unable to find any property that suited their needs. 'There are a lot of fees related to establishing a SMSF. So if they can't find a property to buy (you never know), then this SMSF will be established for nothing,' the paraplanner said. It was also the paraplanner that documented the impact of the cost of insurance premiums on the couple's superannuation funds. Insurance, the paraplanner suggested, should only be entered into once the property and SMSF were established. 'The recommended insurances is costing $22,524 per annum inside the self-managed super fund which is a big chunk of the $200,000 balance. If they are considering to buy a property down the track, this large insurance premium may affect their ability to service the loan,' the paraplanner said. 'They could make additional contributions to super to service the loan but they haven't got much surplus funds outside super at all. This is another reason why they should consider the insurance after the property is found and review the whole situation together to ensure the whole thing (buying a property and getting cover) works without any cash flow issue within the SMSF.' The paraplanner had cast doubt on the appropriateness of setting up the legal shell that is an SMSF and insurances if there was no property to drop into the SMSF box for the sole purpose of growing the funds available to the couple for retirement.

There would be a financial impact on the financial planner's level of remuneration if a transaction were undertaken in one month or another given the way in which the rewards or bonus system worked. It should be noted that the paraplanner recommended no SMSF be set up nor insurance sold to the couple until such a time as a property was found. If the paraplanner's advice had been followed, no insurance product sales would have been made if no suitable property was found for their business. Evidence of Westpac's reward scheme was tendered to the commission and it specifically noted that the advisers had their base remuneration and variable remuneration. The latter was based on their ability to generate revenue on a monthly basis and that means adding sales to the bottom line.

Questions were asked of BT Financial Advice's national head, Michael Wright, about the financial performance targets advisers were required to meet as well as being quizzed on the specifics of the advice in the McDowall case. Wright presented the BT Financial Group's evidence related to the conduct of planners in two specific cases, which included the advice given by Mahadevan to the McDowalls. Throughout his evidence, Wright emphasised that the strategy that was put in place for the McDowalls was unviable. 'It's very clear that this was not a viable strategy for the McDowalls, and I'm sure the McDowalls were passionate and excited about what their future could look like but the reality was it wasn't viable, and at that point in time, as professionals, as Mrs McDowall stated, we should have made it very clear this is not viable. It was poor advice.'

Wright suggested that Mahadevan could have used other means to explain the fact the strategy was unviable to the McDowalls who had their hearts set on this entrepreneurial ride into the sunset of the lives. 'I think if Mr Mahadevan had spoken about the possibility and gave – given, sorry, the McDowalls alternatives right in that first meeting, had offered to do some cash flow analysis, what-if scenarios and help them see that, maybe this is not viable as much as you want it.'

SHOPPING FOR PROPERTIES

Properties that met the general suggestions made by Sleiman were difficult to come by and the McDowalls kept searching for properties that would suit the investment vehicle they wanted to use. They had presented Sleiman with a Beechworth property they had been looking at for some guidance during the first meeting with Westpac. 'The information showed that the property was advertised for about $1,400,000 and had separate room inside for B&B guests and a management area out the back,' McDowall's witness statement explained. 'It was beautifully decorated with French décor. Karl said that the assets were worth more than the property and we couldn't purchase the assets through an SMSF.'

There was a meeting on 17 November 2015 during which the McDowalls discussed properties that may be suitable for purchase as a part of their retirement plan. 'One was in Lakes Entrance, which consisted of a private property for us to live in, and it had seven two-bedroom cottages,' McDowall told the hearing. 'The other one was in a place in Victoria called Bright, so they were both in Victoria, and that was just one home which had a three-bedroom house for us to live in and it had another five rooms that we could let out as a bed and breakfast.'

They were told by Sleiman that the Lakes Entrance property was on two titles and was unsuitable for the purposes of an SMSF. The other property in Bright was also ruled out by Westpac despite the fact that the property was on one title.

The course of events confused the McDowalls who had assumed that they would be able to purchase a property that had a single title with a loan. They had by this stage already sold their home and were living in rental accommodation with the hope that the issue of a bed and breakfast would be resolved as soon as practicable. The couple were not only told that they were unable to purchase either property but that the bank was unable to lend them an amount greater than $200,000 for the purpose.

'So at that time I got really – a little bit upset and a little bit emotional, and I said, "This has just been a complete waste of time. We went through all this for five, six, however many months it is, and you're now telling us that from being able to borrow two million that we can't even borrow 200,000",' Jacqueline McDowall told Orr. 'So at that time I said, "There's no way that we can do that strategy and the goals and the advice that we gave you because there's no property out there that's ever going to be – that you can buy that we're going to be able to do that from".'

Mahadevan suggested that they could contemplate buying an investment property as a part of their retirement strategy. 'I said, "Well, I don't think that that makes any sense". I said, "We sold our family home on your advice. We now don't have a family home to live in. So why would we then buy an investment property to rent to someone else when we haven't even got a property to live in our self?"'

The McDowalls went home and then thought about what to do next. 'The plan was for everything to go towards the B&B and we had been so excited about it. We shared our excitement when we told our family. Now we felt stupid,' McDowall said. 'It was embarrassing. We no longer had a house nor any prospect of pursuing our retirement goal. We didn't want to tell our families that we had received bad advice and our plan was off.' It was at that point that the McDowalls resolved to complain about the advice they had received from Westpac.

MCDOWALLS ON THE WARPATH

The couple chose to represent themselves when they went on the warpath against Westpac and what they felt was inappropriate advice that had cost them a significant amount of money. They first took their complaints to Westpac and the complaints handling process at the bank did not give them much satisfaction. The couple met with Westpac staff responsible for handling complaints and they received a mixed reaction. One Westpac banker reviewed their file and said the strategy was never going to be viable and the bank would never have loaned them the money required for the establishment of the bed and breakfast business. A contrary perspective was encountered by the McDowalls in a second meeting called to look at the financial advice they had received. Another Westpac banker argued that the strategy may still be viable. 'The complaints process was very hard and stressful. We had to go over the same information every time we spoke to a new person,' McDowall told the commission in writing. 'It made me feel like a criminal, like I had done something wrong but all I did was seek financial advice.'

The couple found the first offer of compensation made to them, in a letter received in February 2016, underwhelming. A meagre sum of $17,988.46 was offered. That amount was said to be for reimbursement of advice costs, insurance premiums, storage unit costs and interest that was lost during the process of structuring an investment plan for a bed and breakfast that never materialised. A second compensation amount was put before the couple as a way of resolving the complaints against Westpac but the $50,988.40 was still not satisfactory. Westpac staff told the couple that the amount they were being offered would be as much as what the complaints resolution managed by the ombudsman's service would give them. The McDowalls refused to accept the higher amount from Westpac and went to the ombudsman's service for further action.

MCDOWALLS VERSUS WESTPAC

It was the ombudsman's processes that were to finally see the McDowalls achieve some degree of justice in the aftermath of the battle with the banking giant. They found the process difficult and Jacqueline McDowall noted that the couple would be faced with process delays because new case officers would be assigned to their dispute and they would need to provide the documentation that was already lodged with the ombudsman's service again. 'On 27

February 2017, FOS made a recommendation that Westpac pay us $79,322.08,' McDowall said. 'We did not accept the recommendation because we still didn't feel this was enough to compensate our loss and we didn't feel it would put us back to where we were in the first place. We wanted a final ruling from FOS.'

It was their second attempt for what they saw as justice that brought the McDowalls some degree of comfort. The second hearing at the ombudsman's service resulted in the couple receiving a payout that they were happier with and would be able to move on. 'On 17 August 2017, FOS made a determination in our favour. The finding was that Krish should have advised us that the strategy to purchase a bed and breakfast was not realistic in our circumstances,' McDowall said in her statement to the royal commission. 'FOS found that Krish's actions caused loss as we would not otherwise have started the strategy, sold our home or purchased the level of life insurance that Krish recommended. In addition, we would have retained our existing superannuation arrangements.' The couple received $107,475.18 following the second determination from FOS, which was an amount infinitely greater than the $17,988.46 first proffered by the bank as an adequate amount to resolve the concerns of Jacqueline and Hugh McDowall.

OTHER COSTS OF THE WESTPAC SAGA

The McDowalls kept the financial distress to themselves and they felt embarrassed by the whole episode with Westpac. Family members were told when the couple were planning to get the venture up and running. They had kept the rest of their angst from family and only revealed what they had gone through when they were getting themselves ready to tell their story before Commissioner Hayne in order to share their experience so others wouldn't go through the same thing. 'I first told my daughter the night after I got the telephone call from the royal commission to ask me to appear, and I told my daughter what was happening, where I was going and she says, "Mum, why

didn't you tell us? There is nothing for you to be embarrassed about",'
Jacqueline said. 'And I've only then told my son who is in the UK at
the moment with his family. And, again, they said, "There's nothing
for you to be embarrassed about, you went for financial advice, and
you were led up the garden path which is absolutely awful".'

FROM TV TO OBSCURITY

||||||||||||||||||||||||||||||||||||||||||||||||

'I would have lost a half a million dollars if I had used Henderson Maxwell, and that would have been just for starters.'

DONNA MCKENNA IN EVIDENCE TO THE COMMISSION

'I do not accept that a financial adviser can avoid responsibility for defective advice by claiming the advice is a draft.'

COMMISSIONER KENNETH HAYNE

SAM HENDERSON had it all as a high-profile financial adviser. He was the chief executive officer of Henderson Maxwell, a firm that bore his name, and a host of a Sky News Business program that offered financial advice to people. His media presence, which also included opinion pieces on finance published in newspapers and magazines, was thriving and clearly it was being noticed by potential clients such as Donna McKenna, a Fair Work Commissioner seeking advice to refine her retirement plans. It took his appearance before the Hayne Royal Commission, following a submission made by McKenna that trawled over inappropriate advice given to a highly financially literate client, to see years of building an advisory practice end within months. It was the case study that featured Henderson that highlighted the dangers for clients of financial advisers who had little financial knowledge accepting a financial strategy that could cost them a large amount if they were unaware of the implications of the transactions they were authorising to take place. It would not have been in Henderson's crystal ball at the start of 2018 that the firm that bore his name would disappear within months after he delivered his evidence at the royal commission. He sold his stake in his firm and retreated from a profession for which he had become such a public face. The practice merged with another firm and Henderson Maxwell was consigned to history.

FIRST CONTACT

Valentine's Day in 2018 will be remembered by McKenna as the day she first contacted the royal commission in order to raise concerns she had about advice given to her by Sam Henderson in late 2016. She told the commission that she had sought to contact Henderson for advice in part because of his high media profile. She knew that he had a regular presence on Sky News Business and that he wrote articles that featured in the *Australian Financial Review*. His firm had also won the Association of Financial Advisers Practice of the Year Award, McKenna noted, and she called Henderson Maxwell to arrange for a discussion about her financial affairs on 3 November 2016. Her initial call to the practice seeking an appointment also involved a brief phone interrogation so that the Henderson Maxwell staff member was able to pass some key details to the boss. McKenna received a phone call from Henderson that same day and she let him know that she was seeking financial planning advice because of superannuation law changes that were effective from 1 July 2017 and there was a property purchase playing on her mind. Henderson also told McKenna that there was an electronic questionnaire they required her to fill in that would build on her personal details that were already discussed. McKenna told Henderson that she did not want to complete an electronic form and she was unable to fill in specific details such as regular expenditure. Henderson told her to enter anything in the expenditure fields – he suggested $1,000 a week – and estimates in the fields for current balances. These numbers, Henderson told McKenna, would get checked later on. A meeting would be held between Henderson and McKenna within days of the first phone conversation.

The adviser and client met on 7 November 2016 and McKenna brought other financial particulars with her to assist with the discussion. These included her remuneration package and other matters that any financial planner will want to understand before considering the provision of financial advice. What is significant to this case is the additional questions that Henderson asked McKenna during that meeting as set out in McKenna's witness statement. He asked her whether she might be interested in shares and her response was that recommendations for some blue chip shares would be welcome. There was also a question attempting to gauge her interest in managed investment funds through Henderson Maxwell. McKenna said she may be interested but that she would want to see comparative information related to fund performance. Henderson then asked McKenna about whether she had any interest in self-managed superannuation funds. McKenna's interest in self-managed vehicles was non-existent and she told the celebrity planner she 'liked having my superannuation in large Government-related superannuation funds, particularly given their very low costs to me as a member'. She further told the commission under examination by Orr that Henderson pressed her on the issue of establishing an SMSF using Henderson Maxwell's services, persisting even though she had expressed her reluctance.

'I was almost laughing at him at this stage. I said, "Sam, I probably would go bankrupt if I had a self-managed superannuation fund. And then I wouldn't only be bankrupt, but I wouldn't have a job either",' McKenna said. 'And I explained some of the reasons, in brief form and in a self-deprecating way, that there are only certain circumstances whereby a statutory office holder can be removed from statutory office.'

Her explanation of why she did not want to entertain the establishment of an SMSF did not deter Henderson from continuing to press her on establishing an SMSF. She later agreed to receive information related to the establishment of an SMSF. It was this portion of the initial face to face meeting that would become important throughout the dispute that subsequently arose between Henderson and McKenna related to the quality and propriety of the advice given to this client. It was also during the first meeting that Henderson told McKenna the advice would take some time to prepare. She took it as a sign of thoroughness and an indication that the advice will be tailored to her needs as discussed. Some of the methods used to get an understanding of her financial situation would later surprise her.

IMPERSONATING THE CLIENT

Henderson Maxwell had a staff member that decided, according to the evidence presented to the royal commission, to do the research required to understand McKenna's financial arrangements by calling the Fair Work Commissioner's superannuation fund and posing as McKenna. There were six such calls made by the staffer and the calls were tendered by Orr as a part of the hearings dealing with inappropriate financial advice. Orr asked Henderson to listen to the phone calls and he acknowledged that the calls were made by a staffer from his now defunct firm. The purpose of inquiries was to ascertain what McKenna's financial arrangements were and what precisely she could do with the funds in her superannuation plan. A submission from Henderson to the royal commission noted that he did not become aware of the deception that took place during those phone calls until 28 April 2017, which was the date on which he was told about the recordings by the FPA as a part of a disciplinary investigation. Henderson told Orr during the hearing that he was disappointed and apologised for the staff member's behaviour. He was persuaded to not terminate the staff member by one of his colleagues despite his first instinct being to sack the staffer for misrepresentation.

'I wanted to terminate her employment. I took counsel with my general manager at work. He convinced me not to terminate her employment. Instead, we gave her a warning. It was borderline,' Henderson said. 'In hindsight, I should have persisted with my gut reaction, which was to terminate her. I feel that I would have – and should have done that. We are a small team. It is like a family situation in there on a day-to-day basis, and we felt that the impact would be significant on the business and on the rest of the staff.'

Henderson ended up making a call to the relevant superannuation fund in which McKenna had the monies that he was suggesting she roll over into a self-managed vehicle to understand what the financial situation was for McKenna.

A SELF-MANAGED SUPERANNUATION FUND?

To McKenna's surprise the Henderson Maxwell crew got back to her in what seemed to be record time. Henderson sent her a request for a brief meeting to present a statement of advice. She got an even greater surprise when she was presented with the statement of advice by Henderson during the meeting at which her son was also present. A self-managed fund was at the centre of the plan presented by Henderson on a projector screen. 'Although I had agreed that Mr Henderson could include any recommendation on a self-managed superannuation fund as one option for my consideration, the advice he presented to me on 14 December 2016 relevantly (I was later to read in the Statement of Advice) included only one option,' McKenna noted, 'being that I roll-over my SASS superannuation into a self-managed superannuation fund to be managed by Henderson Maxwell.' McKenna was also concerned that Henderson had failed to provide her with a comparative analysis of the performance of managed investments portfolios managed by Henderson Maxwell before recommending a specific investment vehicle. She told Orr during examination that she thought the advice was 'risible'. 'And I can remember saying to my son words to the effect, "I can't believe this.

I've been to see the financial planner of the year and this is what you get",' the Fair Work Commissioner said. 'I said to my son I thought that if I went to an independently owned financial planning firm that I wouldn't be subjected to product flogging of the type associated with the big banks and, yet, all I'm being flogged is Henderson Maxwell's own products and services.'

Buried down the back of the statement of advice was the kicker. Henderson Maxwell outlined the costs of the arrangements being proposed for McKenna. She was concerned about the fees that were detailed in the statement of advice as she was in a low-cost superannuation arrangement within the public sector. Initial charges for financial planning advice totalled $11,035, which was made up of a $4,950 plan preparation fee, a $1,980 establishment and an initial $4,105 in brokerage fees. These charges related only to kicking off the plan as presented by Henderson Maxwell. McKenna would have had to shell out an estimated $14,642.97 on an annual basis in order to engage Henderson Maxwell to monitor and maintain her financial arrangements on her behalf.

Henderson on the other hand told Orr during examination at the royal commission that he took a different vibe from the first meeting in November 2016. He told the commission that he believed the advice was consistent with what was discussed with McKenna, referring to the fact that the area in which he had developed an expertise is SMSF advice. '[I] felt we had a reasonable discussion around having a self-managed super fund. And this was supported in both my contemporaneous notes and also her annotated notes on the statement of advice that she sent back to me on 9 January 2017. She said she didn't recall having a discussion around it, but she would consider it,' Henderson told Orr at the hearing. He further reinforced that he felt that they had 'discussed what those options were and that we had collectively come to the agreement that a self-managed super fund was suitable for Ms McKenna'.

McKenna and Henderson had a robust exchange when they met after she had time to digest the full implications of the proposals placed before her. She gave it to him with both barrels, according to the evidence given to Orr during examination. 'If I had followed your advice, I would have lost a half a million dollars. You're supposed to be the expert. I don't profess to be an expert in superannuation and retirement planning, or words to that effect,' McKenna noted. 'But even I can read what's written in a members' statement. So I said, "how could this have happened?" Mr Henderson said it was the para-planners. I should interpose to say I didn't know what paraplanners were. I thought they might be akin to paralegals. And I said what are paraplanners?' It was made clear to McKenna that other staff had been involved in researching aspects of the intended plan. Henderson, under questioning from McKenna, acknowledged the ultimate result of the plan as drafted by him for her was for all of her money to be managed by Henderson Maxwell. McKenna did not buy the sales pitch and Henderson offered to repay the money for the preparation of the Statement of Advice. This was an offer McKenna asked to be put in writing and Henderson sent an email as requested shortly after the meeting. A complaint was lodged by McKenna with the firm on 17 January 2017 and McKenna received an apology from Henderson as well as a refund of the advice fee shortly afterwards.

OFF TO THE DISCIPLINARY PANEL

As a member of the FPA, Henderson was the subject of the professional body's disciplinary regime that can deal only with the conduct of the member within the context of the organisation's rules. This means that a member of the FPA or other professional body is only able to be removed from membership. It is nothing unusual, mind you, because professional bodies have only one ultimate sanction: expulsion. There are other sanctions that might be publication of the member's name in a journal; an order that they undertake further professional education on a specific matter of law or practice the member has been found non-compliant in; and a financial penalty such as a fine or the meeting of costs of holding a hearing. This is typical of professional associations that have constitutions and bylaws that specify the conduct that is deemed acceptable by the membership body. What is either ignored or not understood by some people is the fact that there are often privileges that are given to professional organisations in law that are extended to members of their body. There are laws that allow certain professionals to sign statutory declarations if they are members of certain organisations. The professional accounting bodies such as CPA Australia and the Institute of Public Accountants, for example, fall within this category. Expulsion from a professional body also means that a person who could previously sign certain kinds of documents as a member of the professional accounting body is unable to fulfil a statutory function for clients. The professional bodies have an extra-legal role in regulating their membership but this only excludes an individual from being a member of an organisation recognised under law. The removal of statutory registrations or bans from practice are dealt by regulatory bodies. This does not mean the disciplinary processes of member bodies have no practical consequence to the person that is expelled. Expulsion does mean that members are constrained by what they are able to do in circumstances where member conduct falls outside an ethical code or is deemed to be conduct that brings their organisation into disrepute. The latter is a catch all in case the member has done something illegal or untoward that may not be strictly related to professional duties. It gives the professional organisation some flexibility should the organisation decide a member and any incidents in which they have been involved may harm the reputation of the association.

McKenna lodged a complaint about Henderson's advice to her to the FPA in March 2017 and the case was first investigated by Mark Murphy, the investigating officer at the professional body. Murphy was McKenna's main point of contact as the investigations officer for the FPA. Investigations officers will liaise with both parties to ensure that they provide the necessary statements and evidence so that the merits of a case may be evaluated and proceed to a further stage of disciplinary action should the complaint be found to have substance.

The investigator reported back on the issues related to the statement of advice and pointed to the fact that it was unlikely the advice met the tests required for client benefit. Murphy's report noted that there was a 'strong and reasonable inference that the member's conduct stemmed from a lack of objectivity or a conscious decision to place his own interests before those of the client'. Murphy was referring to the fact that the recommendations were all aligned with activities Henderson and his firm were involved in rather than being investments or vehicles that might have met McKenna's initial request for information about a broader range of products. 'It is not apparent that the member would not have made the same recommendations if not for his conflicts,' Murphy said in a 26-page brief to the FPA's disciplinary body, known as the Conduct Review Commission, that was tendered as an exhibit to the royal commission. 'It is not apparent that the Member based all judgements on the complainant's relevant circumstances.'

Henderson decided to provide negative character references for McKenna on more than one occasion in his correspondence sent to Murphy during the disciplinary process. He described McKenna's written response to Murphy as being 'dismissive, comprehensive to the extreme and highly disconnected from any personal relationship'. Henderson goes further. 'She has been described by the press as the "Nitpicking Commissioner" and acting as the "Devil's advocate" by Barrister Stuart Wood in her role as a Commissioner at the Fair Work Commission,' said Henderson in correspondence to Murphy sent in May 2017. In a subsequent email dealing with the disciplinary matter, Henderson requests that Murphy keeps the character references confidential and to not share them with McKenna. He later acknowledged that it was inappropriate to make such references to a former client in correspondence with an investigating officer looking into the case when pressed under cross-examination by Orr.

Henderson also wrote to contact Dante de Gori, the FPA's chief executive officer, expressing concern about the speed at which the investigation was proceeding. Those emails were tendered to the commission and revealed that Henderson appeared frustrated at the speed of the process, which was also a concern expressed by McKenna in correspondence with the investigating officer Murphy. Henderson told de Gori that he was disappointed with the process after his many years of support of the FPA 'but whilst I've tried being open and honest about the situation, I'm afraid my support for the FPA is at a conclusion'. Henderson said Murphy appeared to have his own agenda and that there was 'zero support for members' and further tells de Gori 'my peers would be interested in the workings of this process and what it means to be a member of the FPA'. De Gori told Orr during the hearings that he did not respond to that email sent by Henderson as he did not agree with Henderson's description of the disciplinary regime. 'I take a lot of pride in the fact that we do have rigorous processes. And it's not meant to be an easy process in terms of going through the disciplinary process,' de Gori said. 'It is, obviously, confronting, there is a complaint against you. And members may feel defensive as a result of that. So if it is a difficult process, well, then that's actually a good thing.'

THE FINAL OUTCOME

McKenna first reported her concerns about the advice provided to her by Henderson in March 2017 but the matter had dragged on through the FPA's administrative plumbing for various reasons and an outcome was not finalised and publicly announced until 11 October 2018. De Gori told Orr during her grilling of him during the hearings that there were several matters that led to the delay in finalising the high-profile disciplinary matter. Investigating officer Murphy resigned from the FPA in late 2017, which meant the matter needed to be handed over to another person for management. There were also negotiations with Henderson that related to the nature of the breaches of the disciplinary code that also involved a law firm acting on Henderson's behalf. The FPA announced the matter was resolved and that Henderson was found in breach of its professional rules.

Nine out of ten alleged breaches were proven, according to a media release issued by the FPA on 11 October 2018. The 24-page decision of the Conduct Review Commission, which contains an analysis of each breach based on the McKenna complaint, reveals that Henderson was fined a total of $50,000 and that the breaches of the FPA's rules that were proven were not minor in nature. Henderson's exit from the financial planning sector is noted in the report of the commission because it was the McKenna matter and his appearance before the royal commission that led him to cease his financial planning career. The panel deciding on the case took great pains to note 'it has not taken into account in its consideration in any adverse way the appearance of the member at the royal commission, as it is not relevant to the conduct of the member found to be in breach and for which the sanctions herein are being imposed, but it has noted the explanation given'. This disciplinary ruling by the FPA's panel was cited in the royal commission's final report and it was noted that it was unclear how a $50,000 fine might be recovered as neither Henderson nor his firm were still within the financial planning sector.

The interim report of the royal commission gave the FPA's disciplinary regime a dressing down with Commissioner Hayne describing the process as one that 'did not encourage great confidence in FPA's disciplinary arrangements, at least as they stood when the commission took evidence about the matter'. Commissioner Hayne said. 'The process described in evidence was prolonged, opaque and directed more to settling an agreed outcome to the complaint than imposing proper standards of conduct by members.'

The interim report further observed that Henderson's decision to not renew his membership mid-way through the disciplinary action would not mean much if the consequence was expulsion from membership because the member under investigation had already made the decision to leave. The royal commission's final report recommended a new statutory disciplinary structure that would force registration of financial advisers and also enable the loss of an adviser's meal ticket – the statutory registration – if they were found to have breached the law or relevant standards of practice. This does not mean member bodies are off the hook, however, because no member body can contract out its obligation to take action against its members when they fail to meet the standards expected by professional bodies themselves.

ASIC BANS HENDERSON FOR THREE YEARS

The corporate regulator announced that it took action in July 2019 to ban Sam Henderson for three years from providing financial advice, which is more than a year after Henderson gave evidence before the royal commission. ASIC found during what it called 'surveillance work' that Henderson had failed to act in his client's best interests. He also failed to provide appropriate advice and didn't place a priority on their needs.

'ASIC also found that Mr Henderson did not properly document or investigate his clients' existing products, failed to provide advice that was relevant to their specific goals and recommended the use of in-house Henderson Maxwell products without providing product comparisons or justifying why the in-house products were better than his clients' existing products,' the corporate plod said.

The media release announcing the three-year ban, which has little practical effect given that Henderson vacated the financial advisory pitch, also advised punters that Henderson still may not be out of the woods. 'ASIC's investigation,' the release noted, 'into Mr Henderson's conduct is continuing.'

DEBT-LADEN IN DEALINGS WITH CAR LOAN

||||||||||||||||||||||||||||||||||||||||||||||||

*'Ms Thiruvangadam's experience and the instances
of misconduct relating to car finance disclosed
in Westpac's submissions demonstrate that the
fear of potential termination does not always
inspire compliance with processes by all dealers.'*

COMMISSIONER KENNETH HAYNE

*'Westpac accepted that the loan to Ms Thiruvangadam
"should not have been approved".'*

COMMISSIONER KENNETH HAYNE

CAR DEALERSHIPS SELL CARS but they also open the
door for clients to access loans and insurance products at the point of
sale. This process may work in cases where customers buying a car are
in a position to pay the loan or insurance costs. It gets ugly when a
customer is unable to make payments because their creditworthiness
is misrepresented by an agent acting on behalf of a bank.

This was the experience that confronted Malaysian-born Nalini
Thiruvangadam when she sought to get a replacement vehicle so she
was able to get to work and drive her children around. She came to

Australia almost twenty years ago on a student visa to study to become a personal care attendant. She worked full-time in her field of choice until August 2011, in what she describes in her witness statement as a high care facility. She was appointed a coordinator for a low care facility before working as a casual home care assistant for 21 hours a fortnight for a modest salary. Additional shifts were offered from time to time and she worked those when they became available. She also received a single parent payment as well as other allowances from Centrelink but this did not mean the household was coping. There was also assistance from her family. This was a household that was experiencing financial difficulty. TAFE studies in pathology were also being undertaken by Thiruvangadam but this had not led to work. There was a serious injury that arose from a fall in September 2012 and she was unable to work from that time. Centrelink became her only source of income. How did a woman struggling to meet ends meet end up getting a loan for a car and as a result enter into a fight with one of Australia's big four banks?

CAR CAUGHT FIRE

It was during 2011 that the family car, a Mitsubishi Magna used to ferry her children to and from school, suffered fire damage. While the car was not a write-off, according to the mechanic, it was certainly unreliable and Thiruvangadam needed to consider buying a new car. 'And the reason why I have to buy a car is because I need to pick my kids and drop my kids to school,' Thiruvangadam said. 'And also at that time I was working. I need a car to go, like from home to home to look after elderly residents.' It was at this point that the single mother began to try to secure finance from banks but she found it difficult. This was partly due to the fact that lenders were raising questions about her credit history. She first went to Westpac but the conversation with a staff member produced no fruit. 'Well, she went through a few questions and then she asked me to hold on and then she came back on the phone, like, after one or two minutes and she said that, you know, "I'm sorry at this stage I can't approve your loan because it looks like you have some credit problem". And then she asked me to call the credit office to find out the history,' Thiruvangadam explained. The credit problem appeared to be a Citibank credit card on which money was owed. Other banks were called. Phone calls were made to the Commonwealth Bank, ANZ, the National Bank and various finance companies. These companies were also roadblocks because Thiruvangadam was confronted by the same problem. Her credit history was the roadblock but this did not dampen her enthusiasm for the hunt. She needed a car.

A car purchase did eventuate but the source was some distance away from where Thiruvangadam lived. She told the royal commission that she contacted a car dealer after searching online for bank and finance company details. '[The car dealer is] about 50 kilometres away from my house and I called the car dealership and spoke to the staff and she put me through to the manager in charge,' she said. 'And then when I spoke to the manager, I explained myself, that I tried to call several banks, major banks, and they didn't approve my loan, and also I did call finance and car dealers around my area, none of them approve. And he said, "Don't worry, you come to my car dealer, and you are definitely going back with a car tonight".' Thiruvangadam was uneasy about the relative ease with which the manager of the car dealership had said she would leave their dealership with a car and she made that point directly to the dealer in a phone conversation. 'Well, I told him, "Look, I've called several places, major banks and finance, and other – they all said rejected. I don't want to drive all the way to that particular place, about 50 kilometres away, as I said, and – unless I know I will – if you are going to tell me the answer that no, after me arriving there, like you said, no, your loan has not been approved." So he say, "No, no, you don't have to worry about that. I can tell you right now, you will definitely go back with a car".' She told the royal commission that she understood from the conversation with the manager of the dealership that she would be looking at a new car because she needed one for work and family reasons.

The dealership was in unfamiliar territory for Thiruvangadam so she asked a friend to accompany her to the dealership. It was late when they arrived with the dealership about to close. The manager, however, was accommodating, took her into his office and began speaking with her about her income in order to better understand her financial situation. She brought some evidence of her earnings with her such as payslips and told the manager she received some money from her uncle from time to time to assist with living expenses when things got tight. The manager of the dealership also asked her for expense details and she referred to her $1,500 credit card debt that she had that was not yet paid. 'I also told the manager again that I lived in rented accommodation with my sons, and that I had to pay rent,' she said. The dealership manager also took the details of a Westpac bank card for a direct debit request service agreement and he gave her a copy of this document. Car insurance was also sold as part of the deal. Thiruvangadam already had car insurance with Allianz and that was her first port of call but the manager of the dealership had other plans. 'I telephoned Allianz Insurance from the manager's office to tell Allianz Insurance that I was buying a new car. The manager disconnected my phone call with Allianz Insurance by pressing the button to hang up the phone,' Thiruvangadam said. 'The Manager told me that I had to cancel my existing policy and take out a new policy through him, that would also be with Allianz Insurance.' The royal commission was told that the new policy Thiruvangadam was asked to sign up to was more expensive that the previous policy she held with Alliance Insurance. No explanation was given by the manager about the kind of insurance that was being bought nor what the insurance would specifically cover at that time. The dealership manager was typing on the computer during the meeting, Thiruvangadam noted, while the conversation was taking place. Thiruvangadam was asked to sign several documents once they were printed. She told the royal commission there was no time given to read the documentation in the office prior to being asked to sign the paperwork. 'I felt pressured to sign the documents because it was getting late, it was dark outside and my children and my friend were waiting for me,' Thiruvangadam explained. 'At some point during my meeting with the manager he said "you've got the car, you can take it home now".'

NOT A NEW CAR?

Thiruvangadam had just signed the documents for a car but she was not aware that the car was not new until a staff member accompanied her to test drive the car that she had just bought. It was only during this drive that it was revealed to Thiruvangadam that the car she had signed up to buy was a demonstrator model, a car used to drive potential buyers around. This advice from the dealership staff member was confirmed when Thiruvangadam came back home and found she had signed a contract to buy a demonstrator vehicle. The dealership manager provided Thiruvangadam with his contact details, a series of documents related to purchase of the car and he told her that she should make further contact if she required a loan in the future. 'After my conversation with the manager I understood that I had been given a loan for about $21,000, and I knew that my repayments were to be made within five years,' Thiruvangadam said. 'However, I did not really understand anything else about the loan. I did not understand that the manager would be receiving a commission for setting up my loan.' There was no disclosure of commission or bonus payments during the meeting that Thiruvangadam had with the dealership manager nor was there detail supplied about the insurance, which was Ford Motor Equity Insurance. Thiruvangadam declined to take the car home that evening because it was late in the evening and the car was unfamiliar to her. 'We organised that someone from the dealership would deliver the car to me a couple of days later,' Thiruvangadam explained.

Thiruvangadam became extremely concerned when she got home later that same evening and had the opportunity to read through the documents that she had received from the dealership manager. The loan payments per fortnight were an onerous burden and Thiruvangadam could not afford to pay that much given rent and living expenses chewed up most of her incoming funds. 'I was also surprised by how high the interest rate was – I had thought that Ford dealerships offered low interest rates, after seeing promotions by Ford on the Internet, I was also surprised that the car was a used or demo model as I had told the manager that I wanted a brand new car.' Thiruvangadam called the dealership the next day and told the manager she did not want to go ahead with the sale as she wanted a new car and that the loan repayments were of great concern to her. She was told by the dealership manager that she could not say she did not want the car because all of the documents had already been signed. The car, the manager said, belonged to her and she had to take it. The conversations with the dealership manager also ended up with her needing to supply him with further documentation such as a Centrelink income statement. Her new 'old car' was delivered to her by the end of July 2012.

BURDEN OF PAYMENT

While the purchase of the car occurred quickly, Thiruvangadam's focus turned to the problem of loan payment. She had told the dealership manager that she had a credit card debt and outlined her key source of income. The loan documentation received from the car dealership was problematic in the first instance but difficulties began to multiply because Thiruvangadam started to receive letters from the Bank of Melbourne detailing the amount owed and the payment schedule. Loan payments were due on a Monday while her Centrelink payments would reach her bank account on another day during the week. She told counsel assisting that there were serious problems with keeping up with the payments to the loan. The bank did provide her with some relief from having to pay the loan off for a period when she applied for some consideration but that was only for six weeks. Payments for the loan and other household experiences were at times met by family members. 'Every now and then I will go to my uncle's house and he will lend me money to catch up with the payments and I also had my – my brother used to help me,' she said. 'So that's how I used to catch up with the payments and, yes, I was really struggling.' Rental payments were stopped for several months as a result of an understanding landlord. The Bank of Melbourne, however, kept calling her in order to get payment for the loan. The bank threatened to repossess the vehicle if she did not pay on several occasions. 'Sometimes they said... They are coming now to your doorstep and we are going to tow your car away and you have to pay whatever balance is there in full. Like 20,000 straightforward like that.' Thiruvangadam told the royal commission she cried and asked them to not repossess the vehicle because she has children and it was very difficult.

While her repayment issues caused great financial pain there was also a continuing interaction with the dealership from which she purchased the car. There were difficulties with the car that manifested themselves some months after the purchase. She told the royal commission during the hearing that the car was fine for at least six months. 'After that, I had quite a lot of problem. Like, whenever I reverse from my house, it goes to the – there's a main road there, it goes and stop right in the middle of the road. Several times. And the person who is right at the back, he used to get the guy come in ask me, "What's wrong, can I help you?" And then even he try to start, he can't start,' she said. 'Then he said, "I will push." He tried to, like, drive slowly to the side. And then also my son, when I went to pick my boys from the school, it stops right in the middle of the road. It starts to jerk and then it stops like that. Continuously, it was jerking and – so I called the dealer first.'

A phone call to the manager of the dealership did not result in a conversation focused on any fault in the car. The manager did not believe there was anything wrong with the car. 'He just told me straight on my face, "It's your driving, perhaps it's your driving." And I'm thinking I doubt – at one point I doubt myself, maybe it's my driving, but then I just forgot it, I didn't want to say anything. So I started to drive, but eventually every – started – became worse, and then I called them up again,' she told counsel assisting. 'Every time I called from there on, they don't even put me to the manager. They tried to like, you know, they don't return my call, they don't – don't do anything about it. So finally I said, "I can't come to that particular dealership where I bought the car." Can you – can I go to the closest Ford company to get it checked?". A staff member at the dealership from which she had bought the demonstrator model told her to take it to a Ford dealership as she still had an effective warranty. The dealership examined the car and faults were identified. Repairs were made but Thiruvangadam told the royal commission she needed to take the car for some kind of servicing three times a year because of the recurring problem. It was during one of these visits to a dealership that she took the advice to speak with the legal team at Legal Aid in Broadmeadows. Her legal fight against the Bank of Melbourne began when she took Legal Aid's advice to visit Consumer Action Law in Melbourne. She spoke with lawyers at Consumer Action and gave them authority to act for her on 22 August 2017. They commenced the legal fight to get back what they could from the financial institution.

FIGHT FOR REMEDIATION

Trench warfare between a bank and a customer is not uncommon in circumstances where a customer has been the victim of misconduct. Consumer Action began writing to the Bank of Melbourne to seek remediation on her behalf but not before Thiruvangadam had asked for and received a report on the condition of the car she bought from the dealership back in 2012. It was noted in the report that the transmission clutches dragged and caused the vehicle to stall. The Consumer Action lawyers picked up the cudgels once they received the report. Thiruvangadam's lawyers sought the repayment of all monies that were paid to the bank under the contract and there be no further liability for which she is responsible. Letters were written, exchanged and Thiruvangadam learned via the lawyers that her initial application for the loan should never have been approved in the first place because of her credit history. The Bank of Melbourne made two offers to her in correspondence in an attempt to bring her back to the position she was in prior to entering into a loan agreement with the manager of the car dealership. One offer allowed her to keep the car as well as provided her with a remediation payment of $20,000 while the other offer put on the table by the Bank of Melbourne involved them repossessing the car and Thiruvangadam receiving $24,000. Thiruvangadam opted to keep the car and receive the $20,000 payment.

PROBLEMS IN THE REGIME FOR POINT-OF-SALE LENDING

Commissioner Hayne noted the hole in current credit laws that provided car dealers with an exemption in regulations. They are folks that are not required to obtain a credit license like some other people that provided lending services or provide advice related to customers about forms of credit that may be suitable for them. This exemption, however, means that the bank getting referrals still needs to fulfil its obligations as a credit provider despite the fact that the car dealer fulfils a function of getting essential facts for loan approval purposes. 'Westpac accepted that the dealer plays an important role, but faces no regulatory consequences, and that "Westpac needs and requires Dealers to comply with certain responsible lending obligations in order to discharge its own",' Commissioner Hayne noted. Westpac also told the royal commission that it was clear to dealers that a failure to follow the processes set down by Westpac could result in them being dropped off the list of people involved in arranging finance for car buyers. Thiruavngandam's experience, Commissioner Hayne noted, and the various examples of breaches of rules related to car finance presented before the Commission 'demonstrate that the fear of potential terminations does not always inspire compliance with processes by all dealers'. The chief inquisitor of the royal commission posed a question about Westpac's responsibilities in circumstances where the dealer failed to do the right thing. One point reinforced by Commissioner Hayne was that a bank that had car dealers flogging its loans cannot simply avert its eyes and say that the conduct of the dealer was not its responsibility. Westpac argued that the bank ought to be considered to have complied with its duties under the law because it had reviewed the information supplied by the dealer involved in the case and that it could not verify these details for itself. Blaming a dealer in suburbia someplace for providing dodgy information to the bank is not good enough. The bank itself carries the full weight of the legal obligation and must ensure that it is not approving loans for people who are unable to meet repayments. 'It must be recalled that a licensee's responsible lending obligations are non-delegable,' Commissioner Hayne said. 'The subcontracting, in effect of its sales activities to intermediaries cannot be allowed to obscure this fact.'

GOING TO DOVER
NO MORE

||||||||||||||||||||||||||||||||||||||||||||||||

*'The Protection Policy was deceptive because it contained
certain provisions the effect of which were to avoid liability
to compensate clients for any loss resulting from
the advice provided.'*

TERENCE MCMASTER'S LETTER TO CLIENTS ON 12 APRIL 2018

*'[Dover] did not undertake [reference] checks in a timely
fashion and undertook the checks because of ASICs
expectations and not because of an interest in
the outcome of the checks.'*

ROWENA ORR QC, COUNSEL ASSISTING THE ROYAL COMMISSION

DOVER FINANCIAL SERVICES was once a thriving financial advisory practice run by Terence McMaster, also known as Terry,
but it had effectively ceased to exist by the time the final report of
the Hayne Royal Commission landed on Treasurer Josh Frydenberg's
desk. This was not entirely because of McMaster's appearance before
the royal commission that featured his dramatic exit on a stretcher
after collapsing in the witness box while undergoing a grilling from
Mark Costello, the counsel assisting the royal commission. Dover had
been on a collision course with the regulator for a little while before
McMaster's turn at the royal commission because the corporate

regulator had gotten wind of the fact that McMaster was the architect of a client protection policy that was drafted to protect advisers from the legal consequences of inappropriate advice rather than provide genuine protection for clients. It was the corporate cop that had forced McMaster's hand and caused him to write a letter to all of the firm's clients to explain that a document that he – a qualified lawyer, accountant and financial planner – had engineered clauses within it that were unlawful and that Dover would not be relying on those clauses in the event that a client believes they had been poorly advised. The letter to clients, which was posted on Dover's website on 12 April 2018, was the direct result of the ASIC closing in on McMaster's operation once they began investigating Dover during 2017 and that so-called protection policy that was out of step with key provisions in the law regulating financial advice. McMaster's appearance before Commissioner Hayne was exactly a fortnight after the message to clients about the flawed protection policy was uploaded on the website. More meaningful discussions with the corporate regulator about the conduct of the Dover advice business ensued with the corporate regulator shortly afterwards.

The consequences for McMaster and his firm came relatively quickly as ASIC sought to ensure McMaster's evidence to the royal commission would come a mere two months before the firm of which he was the sole director would all but vanish as a result of an enforceable undertaking agreed with the plods at ASIC who had come to the view that McMaster could no longer hold an Australian Financial Service License. The client protection policy, a document clearly benefitting from the use of Orwell's Newspeak in its title, would be the undoing of the Dover enterprise that had grown to 408 authorised representatives that serviced 11,000 clients across Australia. Authorised representatives were told on 8 June 2018 that there was to be no new advice issued by them under the Dover banner and that the business was going to wind down. The doors were formally shut on 6 July 2018 with McMaster and Dover, effectively one and the same given his status as a sole director, agreeing to remain a member of a dispute resolution scheme until at least July 2019. Dover and McMaster were bundled out of the financial planning game and started 2019 facing the prospect of a two-day trial related to alleged breaches of the Corporations Act. And to think that the Dover chief failed to rush off the blocks to respond to an invitation from the Hayne Royal Commission.

TOO IMPORTANT TO RESPOND TO HAYNE

Dover Financial Advisers began its existence as an entity called McMasters Independent Financial Planning in 2007 and it was started by Adrian and Terence McMaster. The firm, which had a business address in Cheltenham, Victoria, changed its name to Dover in 2008 and was one of many entities invited to provide feedback to the royal commission on a range of issues of interest to Hayne's flying squadron. It was the only financial services behemoth approached by the Hayne team to refuse to participate by not responding to an invitation. It was apparently not enough for McMaster and the crew at Dover to be invited to respond to the commission's request to assist in identifying cases of misconduct by Dover or any of its authorised representatives. 'It was phrased in terms of an invitation, which we took as not being in any way mandatory,' said McMaster to his inquisitor, counsel assisting Mark Costello. 'You know, an invitation doesn't require a response. And for no real reason other than that.' Costello suggested Dover declined the invitation. McMaster disputed the characterisation. 'The word decline is strong. A better word is didn't respond,' McMaster insisted. 'We just didn't realise that something greater was expected.' Costello continued to grind through his list of issues after these matters related to the inactivity from Dover on the Hayne invite were placed on the public record.

CUSTOMER PROTECTION POLICY

Consumers would generally expect that they would be entitled to some degree of protection in circumstances where their adviser has failed to follow their obligations under the law. It is like a warranty for white goods you purchase from a department store that might provide some protection from inappropriate advice. Dover had instituted a client protection policy that did not offer much in the way of consumer protection and it was embedded in documents clients signed.

McMaster was extensively probed by Costello on the issues related to the so-called customer protection policy that was constructed in such a way as to minimise liability for inappropriate or poor financial advice before he collapsed and was taken out on a stretcher to a waiting ambulance. The policy, which was withdrawn following interaction with ASIC, created the impression in its title that it was a document a consumer could rely on. All pieces of advice from the Dover authorised representatives were required to mention the policy. Commissioner Hayne found that the policy may have amounted to misconduct in the context of the royal commission's terms of reference because the scope of the exclusions 'could hardly have been more extensive'. 'When read as a whole, it is difficult to identify any circumstance where, if the policy was legally effective, Dover would be liable for the conduct of its authorised representatives,' Commissioner Hayne said.

Civil penalty action was kicked off by ASIC against Dover and the regulator's key contention is that it alleges that Dover misled and deceived from September 2015 when the protection policy was introduced because policy:

■ Contained false and misleading representations as to the rights and protections available to clients;

■ Created a significant imbalance in Dover's and its authorised representatives' rights and obligations compared to those of clients; and,

■ Sought to protect the interests of Dover and its authorised representatives by avoiding liability to clients for poor financial advice.

Officers from ASIC confirmed the case was going ahead during a Senate estimates hearing held on 20 February 2019.

DEFAMATION THREAT TO A CLIENT

It is common practice for clients to state their view or opinion of the manner in which they were treated by a financial institution or an individual adviser when they lodge a complaint with the Financial Ombudsman's Service, or FOS. The client must detail the circumstances as they unfolded and the manner in which advice was provided in their circumstances. The client has no option when they lodge a complaint given that complaints by their very nature are lodged against an organisation or a specific adviser that has been engaged to provide financial advice. There is also a caution in the rules of the complaint resolution processes to financial institutions and financial advisory firms to not threaten people with defamation. McMaster's advisory network sent a letter referring to the possibility of defamation action in the case of one complainant seeking compensation for inappropriate advice. This was commented upon by FOS in a letter related to the conduct of Dover during progress of a specific complaint. 'The applicant claimed that the advice provided was not appropriate nor in our best interests and was incorrect regarding capital gains tax. During the course of the dispute Dover, in a letter addressed to the applicant dated 10 August 2015, outlined that making false complaints about financial advisers can give rise to defamation actions and similar proceedings,' FOS told ASIC in correspondence dated 8 December 2016. 'Allegedly, issued correspondence on 10 August 2015 in relation to the applicant's dispute to her mailing address addressed to the occupant.' FOS said that there was also correspondence issued by Dover to a third party that was not involved in the dispute before the external dispute resolution body. It was also noted by FOS in the same letter to the ASIC that Dover had decided to rescind its membership of FOS, which McMaster told Costello under examination was due to dissatisfaction with the manner FOS resolved a specific matter.

Costello produced an article written by McMaster that appeared on the Dover website on 21 January 2016 in which severe criticisms were made about the complaints resolution scheme that Dover elected to remove itself from. Staff working in the external dispute resolution authority were not spared in the polemic. He characterised the complaints resolution processes operated by FOS at the time of the article's publication being an organisation that was an aggressive consumer advocate rather than being an independent complaints resolution process. McMaster said the dice was loaded against the holders of an AFSL. He pointed to the fact that the holders of the licenses were obliged to be members of a process in order to hold the financial services license but that the process was in his view client-centric. 'FOS says it's not bound by the law, the rules of evidence, industry practice, the contract between the parties or even its own prior decisions,' the article by McMaster said. 'I am not aware of FOS ignoring the law, the evidence, industry practice, the contract of its prior decisions to find in favour of the adviser... that will never happen.'

McMaster also offers an unflattering assessment of the qualifications and professionalism of the staff that were employed at FOS. 'FOS is unique in that inexperienced and unqualified non-professional employees form opinions on what experienced and qualified professionals should have done. With the benefits of plenty of time and hindsight,' McMaster said. 'Could you imagine the outcry if this happened in other professions? Say doctors, or architects?' How did a law degree, McMaster said, equip a lawyer to judge what a financial planner's standard of care should be? 'You would expect FOS to be leading the way here, with a team of university qualified financial planners boasting years of relevant and practical experience in financial planning,' McMaster argued. 'Hard earned hands-on real world experience. Recognised expert practitioners in their field, financial planning. But FOS is not leading the way. No one at FOS fills these boots or fits this bill.' He further said that FOS staff could award amounts to complainants of up to $309,000 and likened it to the kinds of damages awarded by Supreme Court judges that are bound, according to McMaster, to stricter rules of evidence, law and procedure than FOS' legally qualified staff.

Costello tugged hard at this thread of McMaster's rhetorical fabric during examination and asked him whether it also applied to the manner in which Dover's own lawyers reviewed the advice produced by authorised representatives. The counsel assisting pointed McMaster to the fact he promoted legal review of authorised representatives' advice as a risk management feature at Dover but his article attacked legally qualified staff working at FOS. Advice provided by Dover authorised representatives was reviewed by lawyers. Why would Dover bother to have lawyers review documents related to financial advice given by clients given the sole director and holder of Dover's AFSL was dismissive of legal qualifications of staff involved in the work of external dispute resolution at FOS? 'I think you're taking a fairly restricted view of what we say and watering it down a lot. We actually have three levels of review,' McMaster said. 'And, yes, the review team are predominantly legally qualified, who then work full-time in this space reviewing statements of advice.' McMaster said quite a few of the lawyers engaged in the work at Dover are also qualified financial planners and they become quite good at what they do.

RECRUITMENT PROCESSES AT DOVER

The royal commission spent the second set of hearings delving not just into the provision of inappropriate advice but also what happened when advisers were found wanting by their own organisations. McMaster and Dover Financial Advisers ended up being the home for some authorised representatives that had unresolved issues prior to arriving at Dover's doorstep to commence work with McMaster's crew. The three advisers that were taken on by Dover, about whom questions were asked in detail, were Adam Palmer, Julie Hamilton and Koresh Houghton. These three authorised representatives were appointed by Dover despite there being some concerns about advice that was provided by them while they were engaged or affiliated with other financial services license holders. McMaster's statement to the commission about the three in his witness statement was that he had not received any complaints about any advice they had provided to Dover clients since they were appointed as authorised representatives of Dover. Counsel assisting had a series of questions in relation to each of the individuals in order to ascertain what checks Dover had done in order to determine what the professional background of each individual they were taking on was with the licensee that they had each previously worked. Dover only checked the backgrounds of the three advisers once they were within the Dover tent.

ADAM PALMER

Adam Palmer appears across several case studies because Palmer ended up at Dover after having worked with several licensees. He first joined Dover in October 2014 but there was no request for a reference check from Dover to a previous licensee, Genesys, until December of that year. Had Dover checked Palmer's background with Genesys, which is an advisory firm linked to AMP, earlier it may have found that there were a series of questions that were being raised about Palmer's client files. Palmer joined Genesys in May 2013 from Australia Financial Services Pty Ltd, which had restrictions placed on its license as a result of poor adviser conduct. There was a sizeable client portfolio that Palmer had at Australian Financial Services. He was managing funds totalling $30 million and it would have been seen as a prestigious addition to any financial services firm's client base. That world of financial advice spins around numbers and $30 million would have been a nice, round figure in which Genesys would have had immense interest but Genesys failed to conduct its onboarding of Palmer properly. AMP's head of compliance, Sarah Britt, acknowledged they had not done sufficient work prior to appointing Palmer.

Amongst the various issues that were raised in evidence at the royal commission was the fact that Palmer flagged the he was unqualified to provide advice in specific areas on which he intended to advise clients. Nobody at Genesys sought to audit or review his files. None of Palmer's files were reviewed until July 2014. This was 12 months after he began working with Genesys. His July 2014 file audit resulted in the lower possible rating for an adviser working under the Genesys brand. One of the files examined by an auditor concerned advice given to a couple seeking to renovate their home. Palmer's advice for this couple wanting to redo their home was for them to create a self-managed superannuation fund, dump their superannuation into that structure and to buy an investment property. Aside from the obvious question related to how that helps a couple renovate their existing home, there were some other problems with this scenario. Files examined on this specific matter had no evidence of risk appetite on the part of the client, the advice was not within the scope of any accreditation held by Palmer and the advice could be deemed to be advice related to property that was not within his authorisation. Britt accepted that similar concerns about Palmer's advice were raised in nine other clients.

The royal commission heard that the audit conduct on Palmer's files found the adviser had a conflict when advising on matters related to investment property purchases. There was a property business in which Palmer had a 60% ownership interest that was a 'buyers advocate'. Palmer referred clients to this business to receive help with property purchases. Britt acknowledged that concerns about Palmer's background and involvements may have been raised had Genesys been more thorough in vetting. A decision was taken by AMP's Issues Panel, which deals with misconduct matters, to let Palmer go but by that stage Palmer had resigned.

Dover Financial Adviser took Palmer on as an authorised representative in October 2014. Britt was unaware of any approaches from Dover to check out their latest talent acquisition. There was no proactive activity on the part of Genesys that Britt could recall when examined by Orr to alert Dover about Palmer's track record at Genesys. McMaster told Costello during the hearings that there was no reference given to Dover by AMP about Palmer's track record. Asked whether there was anything Dover could have been told that would prevent the appointment of Palmer, McMaster said evidence of fraud or a 'detailed list of significant errors, particularly if, when we looked at those errors, it would be likely that they would recur in the future'. Costello asked whether the poor audit result received by Palmer would impact Dover's decision to take him on as an authorised representative. 'Not necessarily,' said McMaster. 'Because we've learnt that what happens in a situation of an unsupervised adviser who is subject to volume quota KPIs doesn't happen in our environment where we have close supervision and support for the adviser,' the Dover chief said. 'And, indeed, that's the situation that has unfolded here. It's also unfolded in many other similar situations.' McMaster highlighted the fact that there are challenges in asking someone who is running a sole practice for a supervisor when, in fact, they supervise themselves.

JULIE HAMILTON AND KORESH HOUGHTON

The royal commission's counsel assisting also examined McMaster in relation to two other authorised representatives, Julie Hamilton and Koresh Houghton, about whom there were concerns expressed by a previous licensee, Financial Wisdom. Both of these financial advisers were taken on by Dover but they subsequently had bans placed on them as a result of breaches reported to the corporate regulator.

Julie Hamilton copped a three-year ban from the provision of advice from the corporate regulator not long after she joined McMaster's outfit. Hamilton was told by McMaster that she would be appointed an authorised representative of Dover within two hours of her advising McMaster that she was in the cross hairs of her licensee at that time, Financial Wisdom. Financial Wisdom had decided they wanted to report Hamilton to ASIC for a significant breach related to statements of advice. McMaster told Costello that he was unconcerned about Hamilton's problem because it would not have happened under the Dover regime given that, McMaster said, the statements of advice were reviewed twice before they were let out into the wild and that the problem complained of by Financial Wisdom would not occur at Dover. 'The particular issues in concern were expensive premiums, and also a loss of continuity of insurance benefits on transfer to – of clients' moneys to Colonial First State. Now, under our review processes, it's extremely unlikely that those two events could occur,' McMaster said. 'So what was described to me as being the problem I saw more as a supervisory problem, reflecting on the institution, than on the individual.' McMaster represented Hamilton at the ASIC hearing in the lead up to her banning and he told the royal commission that her case was a 'sad story'. The Commonwealth Bank had sought to strike an agreement with Hamilton's client for remediation of a small amount – an amount McMaster said was about $1000 – once the bank had determined there may have been compliance problems with the advice that Hamilton had provided them. 'Julie only had a very small practice. It was best described as a micropractice out in Gippsland. More than half of the clients accepted the money and transferred to another adviser,' according to McMaster.

Koresh Houghton was permanently banned by the ASIC after being appointed by Dover. He was given his wings by Dover as an authorised representative on 22 January 2015 but Financial Wisdom was contacted by letter on 10 February 2015 for a reference check. Financial Wisdom expressed concern about the quality of his advice. In each of the three cases that were subject to examination McMaster had said that the advisers had not had any complaints levelled against them by Dover clients and that Dover's systems and processes would mean that the transgressions that occurred in other situations would not occur at Dover.

Costello's questioning of McMaster eventually secured an admission from the Dover chief that he did in fact get it wrong when two advisers that were eventually banned by the corporate regulator were taken on by Dover. Commissioner Hayne was told by Orr during the summing up of the financial advice round of the royal commission that Dover's compliance with its own policies and procedures was not up to standard. 'Each of those examples [concerning advisers] demonstrates that while Dover had policies in place with respect to the onboarding of advisers and undertook reference checks, it did not undertake those checks in a timely fashion and undertook the checks because of ASICs expectations and not because of an interest in the outcome of the checks,' Orr told Commissioner Hayne.

Dover Financial Advisers letter to clients – 12 April 2018

Dear Client,

I am writing to you regarding advice previously provided by Dover.

This advice included materials incorporated into the advice by a hyper-text link known as the Dover Client Protection Policy (the 'Protection Policy').

The Protection Policy has been withdrawn and replaced by the Dover Client Information Policy, with retrospective effect.

The Protection Policy was deceptive because it contained certain provisions the effect of which were to avoid liability to compensate clients for any loss resulting from the advice provided.

Dover does not and will not rely on these clauses in any dispute because they are unlawful and are voided by the financial services law and the general law.

If you consider the advice provided to you has resulted in a financial loss you should seek independent legal advice or lodge a complaint with the Credit Industry Ombudsman and you should disregard the Protection Policy.

Please do not hesitate to contact me should you require further information about this matter.

Terry McMaster

ASIC ASLEEP AT THE WHEEL?

||||||||||||||||||||||||||||||||||||||||||||||

'My question is simple: has ASIC got the message that the expectations of the Australian people are that you are to lift your game?'
SENATOR JOHN 'WACKA' WILLIAMS

'Loud and clear, Senator. Loud and clear.'
JAMES SHIPTON, ASIC CHAIRMAN

THE THICK TOME known as An Inquiry into the Nature and Causes of the Wealth of Nations was written by Adam Smith in 1776 and it contains within its pages the three functions of government. Smith argued that there were some tasks that governments needed to fulfil. These objectives were to ensure a country was defended from other countries, people within the country were protected from each other and that the government would provide the necessary infrastructure for the benefit of the community that would otherwise not be provided by private entities. It is the second of these objectives that Smith highlights – ensuring people do no harm to each other – that has not been met by successive Australian governments where the enforcement of financial services legislation by the corporate and prudential regulators is concerned. ASIC and APRA have come under trenchant criticism for what appeared to various politicians, victims of bank misconduct, media commentators and professional associations to be a profound failure to act when incidents of misconduct were brought to its attention over an extended period of time. Regulation exists so those that are vulnerable are protected but on successive occasions the regulatory system has been found wanting where the banking sector has been concerned.

Criticism of regulators is to be expected but in the context of misconduct that has taken place in the financial services sector the criticism took a sharper, more cynical turn. It was almost as if ASIC's failure to litigate first was seen as a sign that the regulatory body was complicit in creating a perception that it was a 'soft touch' where the largest corporations in the country were concerned. Transpose on this the fact that various individuals from large banks and other institutions serve or have served on consultative forums run by the regulator. This may create a perception that enforcement outcomes may be lax as a result of bankers and regulators being overly familiar with each other. The use of enforceable undertakings, for example, does result in an enforcement outcome. An enforceable undertaking is an action taken by a regulator, but it does not automatically result in heads on spikes. ASIC chairman James Shipton – who had returned home to Australia from a long overseas stint – bore the brunt of all of the issues that had plagued the regulator in relation to enforcement long before he walked through its front door in February 2018. Both he and other ASIC staff were in the hot seat over a range of issues that resulted in the regulator ultimately being complicit in an environment where critics of the regulator appeared to regard it as being a soft touch and too close to those parties subject to its regulation. This occurred when senior ASIC staff communicated directly with representatives of banks that were being investigated by the regulator on matters of misconduct. The habit of a regulator cutting deals with big companies on enforcement issues was repeatedly questioned during the year-long examination of problems in the financial services system.

Shipton did not appear before the commission until the last round during which policy matters were being discussed. By that stage the corporate regulator had begun to properly confront some of the internal practices that may have compromised enforcement outcomes or created the perception that the regulator's actions in relation to major financial institutions left much to be desired.

THE NEW BLOKE

Shipton began the process of familiarising himself with what went on at ASIC during the time his predecessor, Greg Medcraft, was in the chair and he gradually began to change the system of monitoring and regulating the banks. This process was being shaped by Shipton and his colleagues as the grinding inquisition overseen by Commissioner Hayne explored areas in which the regulator could have performed better in relation to fixing matters. The new chairman of ASIC walked into controversy over ASIC's failure to take high profile legal action against banks with other regulatory tools being used. His first encounter with the inquisitive members of Senate Estimates in 28 February 2018 was to be a light affair for the newly minted ASIC chairman. He had barely gotten his feet under the desk but was able to sketch out the nature of the misconduct Commissioner Hayne was to draw out during public hearings. 'For many of the misconduct issues that we have seen, I think a relevant question to ask is whether we are seeing the right levels of professionalism and industry integrity. For example, in relation to vertically integrated or bundled business models, these businesses usually involve conflicts of interest that the law requires be appropriately managed in order to discourage behaviour that causes harm to consumers,' Shipton told Senate estimates in his first opening address before the committee. 'In my view, managing these conflicts requires a whole-of-firm and whole-of-industry commitment to creating a professional culture that encourages the right behaviour at every level, cascading down from the boardrooms through product manufacturing teams all the way to the front line, the point-of-sale staff.' Shipton also flagged during his first appearance that the regulator was prioritising work using the regulator's behavioural research and policy unit on improving financial literacy.

RESPONDING TO COMMISSIONER HAYNE'S PROBE

The Economics Committee of the House of Representatives quizzed Shipton on ASIC's regulatory work on 22 June 2018 and he tabled a series of documents at the outset to illustrate what progress the commission had made or action that was taken on matters that were case studies highlighted by the royal commission. 'Since 2011, ASIC has obtained 160 criminal convictions, and 19 of them have occurred this financial year. ASIC has completed 140 civil penalty proceedings, and 24 of them have been this financial year,' Shipton said. 'ASIC has banned over 800 people from providing financial services or credit. ASIC has banned over 390 people from being directors. And, importantly for Australians, we have recovered more than $320 million in compensation for consumers so far this year. Since 2011, we have secured compensation of nearly $1.8 billion.' He said that the regulator was prepared to use its regulatory powers to deal with misconduct brought to its attention.

Questions came from committee members about the culture within the Australian financial services sector with Shipton pointing to the need for entities themselves to clean up their soiled backyards from the inside. A speech delivered earlier that year by Shipton focused on the need for financial institutions to change their culture and it was to this speech a member of the committee made reference. 'We are calling on [the industry] to identify and do a wholesale review of where conflicts of interest exist inside institutions and the system more broadly and to deal with them, remediate them and mitigate them,' Shipton said. 'That is an urgent call to action, and that is desperately needed by the system for it to regain the trust and confidence of the Australian public.' The ASIC chair also had the declining levels of professionalism in the finance sector in his sights, highlighting the fact that pursuit of profits has clouded the financial professional's mindset. 'I also called on greater levels of professionalism inside financial institutions and by the men and women in finance. They need to be proud in the execution of a very valuable purpose that finance serves for the community and society.' Shipton told the committee that the regulator had more than 1000 regulatory actions of various kinds under way with 800 surveillances and almost 250 investigations at the time he appeared before the House of Representatives' Economics committee.

CLASHES OVER AMP

A member of that same House of Representatives committee, Matt Thistlethwaite, pushed the corporate regulator's senior officers on one of the more significant case studies that had emerged during the financial services hearings at the Hayne Royal Commission. Thistlethwaite, a Labor member of parliament, pointed to the large number of customers that were being charged for but not receiving advice from advisers at AMP and asked why the corporate regulator had done nothing to warn customers of AMP that this was occurring. The AMP's fees for no service was a sensational revelation at the royal commission but ASIC was already conducting investigations into the conduct of the AMP and its officeholders in relation to various matters. Shipton confirmed that the regulator had already begun sinking its teeth into the AMP matters before the royal commission had made the extensive level of misconduct known to the broader public. 'We have – and we have now said this publicly – an ongoing investigation into AMP that includes the matters that were raised at the royal commission, and of course there is a very limited amount more that I can say in relation to that,' Shipton confirmed. 'So we were not surprised at all – at all – about the confronting matters. They were matters that were a part of a long, sophisticated and still ongoing investigation, which we intend to carry on and carry through.' Further questioning on the AMP matter followed and ASIC officials said that they had been aware of the issues related to the AMP's fee for no service arrangements as well as the other scandals that had gradually made its way across the press as one revelation after another was drawn out of the AMP witnesses. The problem for the corporate regulator, however, is that it is required under the Corporations Act 2001 to maintain confidentiality as it is investigating corporate misconduct but the corporate regulator did issue a statement on 18 April 2018 to provide some insight into the work it was doing on the AMP scandal once the issues were ventilated at the royal commission. ASIC confirmed that it had been:

■ Investigating the AMP fees for no service matter that had caused public outrage once aired at the royal commission.

■ Examining both the fee for no service practices and also misleading statements made by AMP to the regulator.

■ Reading through thousands of documents as well as interviewing AMP staff. The corporate regulator noted that it had examined or interviewed 18 staff members.

■ Working to ensure that customers were paid compensation, and,

■ Warning financial institutions that they needed to cooperate with the corporate regulator and ensure that they are truthful.

Shipton told Thistlethwaite and the committee that it was important for investigators to properly investigate the various instances of misconduct in the AMP case and that the Commission would inform the community when it was able to do so. The commission had issued a series of reports on the financial services sector and the practice of fees for no service, which were referred to during the committee hearing.

MORE DETAILED MONITORING OF THE BANKING SECTOR

One of the criticisms of the corporate regulator was that it was incapable of detecting misconduct and dealing with it sufficiently early.

There was also an emerging culture of non-compliance in some quarters that was creating concern amongst politicians, consumers, the media and ASIC officers. One measure that was considered by Shipton to be worth trying in Australia, to see whether the internal culture of banks would improve, was to have ASIC officers conduct inspections and reviews inside the banks on a regulator basis to ensure banks were dealing properly with their compliance obligations. It is not the first time that the corporate regulator had done inspections of firms of varying kinds. There is a practice of the regulator inspecting audit firms that has the regulator examining the culture of a firm as well as looking at random sets of working papers in detail to determine whether there are any breaches of auditing, assurance or ethical standards as well as whether the auditor complied with obligations under relevant legislation. These reviews have typically found shortcomings in audit work and those are documented in a report that is then used by auditors and others as a basis for improving their compliance with professional rules and regulations. Greater surveillance of the financial services entities was deemed necessary to try and bring a better attitude towards regulatory compliance. The royal commission also exposed multiple instances of poor adviser conduct that was frequently not compliant with an institution's code of conduct and also not compliant with financial services regulation. Shipton told a parliamentary committee hearing on 17 August 2018 that the introduction of what was going to be an in-house regulatory presence has the objective of forcing institutions to reflect on what a regulator will think about decisions and actions of the business. 'If you as a decision-maker inside a financial institution are going to interact more regularly with a senior supervisory officer from ASIC then that will bring regulatory issues – the physicality of the regulator, almost – front of mind,' Shipton said.

The culture Shipton wanted to see grow was one where company officers gave active consideration to what a regulator's view on particular transactions or representations is likely to be rather than an entity have difficulties in dealing with the regulator further down the track. 'What we believe is important is that when decisions are being made inside a financial institution they need to have a diverse range of different inputs. They need to be considering, "What would the regulator think about this decision? What is in the best interests of the consumer or the customer",' Shipton said. The approach underlined by the ASIC chief reflected his belief that there was no real consideration of what the regulator may think about the kinds of behaviour in which people had engaged. 'If you ask me, part of the failures of the financial system in recent years is that that type of thinking, that type of dissonance, that type of questioning was not apparent in the decision-making rooms of financial institutions,' Shipton observed.

INSPECTIONS

ASIC was finally taking the approach of having a cop on the beat that takes proactive action rather than waiting for complaints about institutions to rear their head once damage to a consumer had already been done. Continuous monitoring of financial institutions also plays on the fear of those seeking an opportunity to misbehave that they will be caught and punished more quickly than might otherwise have been the case. These kinds of intense programs cost money and the current monitoring program has between $8-9 million allocated to it; and Shipton told the parliamentary committee that it is 'effectively translates to about 25 people'. 'We believe this is a very good start. We will test and monitor this and, if necessary, we will come back to you and your peers for support for expanding it if we think that it's the appropriate thing to do. But, equally, when I say 25, it's going to be virtual; it's not just going to be those 25 professionals,' Shipton said. 'We will be using different resources from throughout ASIC. Importantly, we are also going to be working very closely with our peer agency, APRA, on this, who we have been keeping in close touch with, because of course they have a prudential supervisory role and responsibility.'

There is a problem for this regulatory David in dealing with the Goliaths of Australia's finance sector. ASIC will be testing the effectiveness of this surveillance process, but the commission was already behind in the human resource stakes. This made it necessary for the commission to use a risk-based method to determine what aspects of banking operations it should review at any point in time. 'We also have to realise that the average population of the big four is about 30,000 people, 'Shipton told the committee. 'We at ASIC have 1,600. So there is a limitation as regards the sheer force of numbers.'

Spending any length of time within a bank could pose a threat to the judgement of staff from the regulator charged with keeping an eye on the banks and their practices. Shipton was previously a regulator in Hong Kong and ran a similar program there. 'I can personally speak from my own experience of running a supervisory team in Hong Kong whereby teams would spend up to a number of months inside a financial institution,' Shipton observed. 'But, again, the learnings of other jurisdictions – particularly the United States – are very important here. Firstly, it's just training people before they go on site for the psychological risks of regulatory capture.' ASIC acknowledged that the skepticism of its investigators or reviewers should not be the first casualty of the war against poor compliance and inappropriate advisory practices of banks. How well this surveillance and monitoring, continuing legal action and unprecedented use of public hearing powers helps restore a culture of compliance in those parts of the financial services sector found wanting remains to be seen.

FINAL OBSERVATIONS OF A GOVERNANCE KIND

|||||||||||||||||||||||||||||||||||||||||||||||

'Ms Orr, it's not possible for minutes to record every single question in a board meeting, and most of the questions are, in fact, very serious questions. That is the purpose of the board meeting.'

CATHERINE LIVINGSTONE, CBA CHAIRMAN

THE HAYNE ROYAL COMMISSION does have broader implications for staff, senior management and boards of directors of companies, associations and other entities outside the financial services sector that have not had much focus from the commentariat. There are lessons embedded within the year-long excavation of banking misdeeds that must be heeded by boards in order to ensure that their processes are robust and problems are dealt with in an appropriate manner. The conduct of and the recording of board meetings will need to be reconsidered for some entities. Evidence given by board members related to the keeping of company records ought to cause boards to think carefully about how to record objections or concerns that arise during board deliberations. Various examples of board minutes, committee minutes and reports found their way into the exhibits as a result of the information gathering powers available to the royal commission. Company officers were also grilled about the content of the minutes, which in its own right was a gruelling process to watch. The interrogations of Catherine Livingston, the chair of the Commonwealth Bank, and Ken Henry, the former chairman of the NAB, during the commission hearings on matters related to board minutes is a case in point. Both individuals faced some brutal questioning on the contents of minutes that was played out in the public square and the fact this can occur either at a royal commission or in a court of law during a court case is a reminder that directors need to ensure they note objections to decisions or policies in discussion and then ask for those to be recorded during the meeting. They will need to ensure that their instructions are followed when the draft minutes are circulated by company secretaries as a part of the process of finalisation of board minutes. This will be vital to ensure that directors protect themselves from an individual standpoint. The first question of the director in a witness stand will be precise, cold and cutting: why was the opposition to a deal, a policy or other matters not recorded in the minutes? Where is the evidence that you, Mr Director, opposed this particular measure or expressed a view against it? An investigator or inquisitor is likely to assume that nothing was done if, in fact, nothing appears on the written record of a meeting that has taken place. Company or association minutes are not written in invisible ink and directors need to ensure their concerns are recorded in the minutes of the entity.

COMPANY SECRETARIES AND THEIR DUTIES

Company secretaries must also increase their vigilance and ensure that they ask board members to ensure that any objections, queries or concerns they want documented are put into the meeting minutes. A company secretary – a key cog in a company's compliance machine – can be the target of blame shifting in a toxic environment if board members or management are looking to preserve their own self-interest. A measure such as ensuring a boiler plate request is embedded in emails to all board members for confirmation that they have had all of their concerns documented appropriately will assist in having an audit trail in place. This is not just for reasons of self-preservation, although that should be sufficient cause for these actions to take place. It is a necessary protocol to ensure the board of directors is prompted to ensure that the most truthful account possible of meetings is recorded. It is not just for compliance with relevant laws of incorporation and consumer protection. There is still great merit in ensuring a company's own history is properly told in company records so it can be referred to by future boards of directors and managers.

THE ROLE OF AUDITORS AND CONSULTANTS

The role of auditors and consultants was not examined by the process overseen by Commissioner Hayne, but it would not be long before the Parliamentary Joint Committee on Corporations and Financial Services would begin the process of conducting an inquiry into audit regulation. The inquiry was in part spurred on by concerns that audit firms providing other services to clients for which they did the external audit of financial statements were impacting on the quality of the audit work being produced. Further fuel was added to the fire when concerns were expressed about whether accounting firm EY was independent when it did a review of the NAB's risk management framework following media coverage in *The Age* and *Sydney Morning Herald* of leaked documents that revealed there were still concerns expressed by then chairman Dr Ken Henry about the potential for further remediation payments to customers as a result of products the bank was selling people. There was also an added impetus that could be attributed to overseas debate with the United Kingdom's Competition and Market Authority having conducted a review of the market for audit services. A final report of the inquiry recommended:

■ Operational split of the four major accounting firm's audit divisions with separate chief executive officers, separate accounts, discontinuation of profit-sharing between the audit practice and other parts of the accounting firm and any promotions or bonuses to be based on the quality of audit work done. This option is in lieu of a split of the audit business of Big Four accounting firms globally.

■ Mandatory joint audits where a major accounting firm would 'buddy up' with a challenger firm and both firms would share the liability for the audit work. 'Challenger firms should work alongside the Big 4 in these joint audits and should be jointly liable for the results. There should be initial limited exceptions to the requirement, based on criteria set by the regulator, focused on the largest and most complex companies,' the authority said. Companies choosing a 'challenger firm' – for that read non-Big Four – to fly solo on an external audit engagement would be exempt from having two firms trawling over its systems and books.

■ Tighter regulation of audit committees by the regulator because they are the ones that appoint, supervise and engage with the external audit firm. This recommendation places the directors of an entity in the firing line given that the audit committee would have to justify to the regulator what it has done in its contact with the audit firm.

■ Five-year review of new measures that are put in place.

A major review of audit regulation following the collapse of Enron and WorldCom in the United States and companies such as HIH in Australia tweaked the rules to try to establish more robust independence rules. There is little that is particularly new, fresh and unexplored in the debate over audit independence, the audit expectation gap, auditing and accounting standards and the manner in which regulators ought to regulate audit firms. That said, there is merit in discussing ideas from overseas to ensure that the marketplace here does not feel the issues are ignored. Commissioner Hayne told the Australian community that there was no need for new legislation in the case of banks. Enforcement, the Commissioner opined, was the key that would unlock the mysteries of how to achieve better conduct. It may well be the case in the context of accounting firms where problems may be detected or exist in specific engagements. The corporate regulator, for example, could conduct greater surveillance of compliance with independence rules that exist within the accounting profession, accounting firms and any other relevant regulations. A regulator is effectively the only party that is able to access confidential documents of accounting firms and clients as a part of regulatory processes. Reviews of this nature done periodically could examine what the nature of other services provided to an audit client are and whether there is any real conflict between the work done by the firm's external audit team on the audit engagement and other services. This is a regulatory responsibility given that the regulations already exist in the form of ethical standards and internal firm guidance. It is clear that ASIC does some work in the area of audit independence but there ought to be a more specific review of compliance with independence rules that act as a deterrent to firms that may entertain offering a service inconsistent with the independence rules. Any examination of these issues must also include the relevant board of directors because they are the folks that ultimately seek the advice or services to be performed. Picking on the auditors and their firms alone would make for a half-baked regulatory strategy.

PARLIAMENTARIANS COULD DO MORE

Poking, prodding and exploring audit regulation is fine but the Federal Parliament can and should do more where monitoring professions that are given privileges under law either via a principal Act or by regulation. Professional accounting bodies, for example, are able to give their members the privilege of witnessing declarations and other similar documents because they are recognised in relevant legislation. Why are bodies such as these not examined in the context of privileges they are able to give their members? It is insufficient for parliamentarians to get excited about specific issues such as auditor independence when they show next to no interest in the fact that these organisations have specific recognition under law. Periodic hearings at which professional bodies are required to explain what they do, how they set their internal rules, what happens when they discipline members and what activities they undertake in the public interest are questions accounting and other bodies recognised under law should get asked by parliamentarians. Bodies such as the Financial Planning Association of Australia, which had a turn at the royal commission during the Sam Henderson case study, would also be called to update the parliament on developments within their standards and disciplinary regime. Supervision of associations ought to take place on a periodic basis given that the parliament has given legislated privileges to these organisations. Responding to a current event or trend in order to be seen to be doing something about a topic area ought to be viewed as inadequate. Parliamentarians ought to view the committee system as being one of the available checks and balances on organisations that play an important part in assisting in the regulation of the market place. Any risk management structure or framework has built within it periodic checks and reviews. Politicians ought to view themselves as part of a broader risk management process in this area of the Australian capital market and the law – it is critical that everybody is kept on their toes and parliamentarians need to play a part irrespective of which groups representing large wads of voters it might upset.

APPENDIX 1

||||||||||||||||||||||||||||||||||||||||||||

How would Hayne's disciplinary body actually work?

FIRST PUBLISHED 8 FEBRUARY 2019 IN CRIKEY

MOST PEOPLE KNOW that there is a naughty corner that professionals get sent to when they have broken their codes of conduct. Even if you're not sure of specifics, you know that somewhere there is a person who has the job of playing Sherlock Holmes and finding out whether an accountant, lawyer or doctor has wronged their client.

There are statutory authorities such as the Tax Practitioners Board, which can remove the registration of a practitioner who has failed to behave in accordance with the code of professional conduct, and private sector associations such as CPA Australia and the Institute of Public Accountants. The latter type has disciplinary rules and committees that enforce them where a complaint from a member of the public is valid.

Royal Commissioner Kenneth Hayne has just proposed adding another one of these bodies to the regulatory framework by recommending a single, central disciplinary system for financial advisers. This followed a litany of cases in which internal disciplinary systems within banks appeared to deal inadequately with advisers doing the wrong thing.

Case in point: the royal commission found that financial adviser Sam Henderson's advisory firm gave advice that would have cost its client, Fair Work Commissioner Donna McKenna, $500,000 if she was not adequately switched on. McKenna complained to the firm as well as the corporate regulator, the Australian Securities and Investments Commission. Nether took action.

Henderson's professional association at the time, the Financial Planning Association, received a complaint from McKenna but the association dealt with the matter confidentially. In the end, a $50,000 fine was imposed on Henderson by the FPA in October 2018 but, as Hayne noted in his final report, Henderson had sold his share of the advisory practice, left the industry and 'it is not clear whether or how the penalty would be recovered'.

Hayne's disciplinary system would seek to correct this by reflecting the structure of other regimes that currently operate. Every financial adviser would need to be individually registered. This is not just to monitor or keep track of them, but also to create a barrier for entry. Registering individuals means that they will need to ensure they meet criteria for registration. In other circumstances this means someone must satisfy minimum education and experience criteria. Registered company auditors, for example, must have practiced in audit for some time and a supervising auditor needs to vouch for that experience. The same is true for registration as a tax agent.

Your registration – and your regulatory obligations – follow you wherever you end up as a registered auditor or registered tax agent and the same will happen for financial advisers.

Individual registration also means that the disciplinary panel can directly deal with the person that created the problem for a client. A financial institution would not be able to bury a problem within its own system and protect a rogue adviser that might be a 'rainmaker' with capacity to earn them decent coin.

Employers holding a financial services license would also be required to report certain types of behaviour, and clients and other stakeholders would be in a position to complain about an adviser's conduct.

A disciplinary process such as the one proposed by Hayne would have greater consequences for an adviser than the processes that currently exist in professional bodies. The worst a professional body can do to a professional that goes seriously rogue is expel a person from being a member. A statutory disciplinary process can neuter an adviser's career by cancelling their meal ticket: the individual registration that they would need to hold under the new regime.

This is, however, a gaping hole in the Hayne recommendation that needs to be highlighted: Hayne has left the final form of the registration and discipline model for the government to nut out with industry.

Hayne did not specify the structure of the regime, instead providing key features he wanted to see. Funding is not mentioned in the recommendation, but it should be a no-brainer that industry should not fund the regime. It should be funded by taxpayers and treated as a serious quasi-judicial forum; the registration of an adviser is a matter of law rather than an industry body membership.

Industry contributions to funding such a structure would conjure up images of 'financial adviser discipline brought to you by the CBA, NAB, ANZ'. You may as well give them billboards outside the offices housing the disciplinary system because industry funding would kill the credibility of the process before it even begins.

APPENDIX 2

||||||||||||||||||||||||||||||||||||||||||

Banks robbing us blind

PUBLISHED ON 29 JANUARY 2019 IN THE DAILY TELEGRAPH

THE FINAL REPORT of the Banking Royal Commission is sure to expose much of the industry's dirty laundry.

Banking customers have about a week to wait for the final report from Commission Kenneth Hayne that is the final deliverable of the year-long process that has brought a critical eye on the ethics, commercial motivations, remunerations schemes and standards of governance of the financial services sector.

That report is expected to contain more critical observations of the performance of Australia's regulators – the so-called protectors of the capital market – and our largest financial institutions in which the maintenance of unquestioning, uncritical blind trust can no longer be afforded.

What the commission has exposed to a bewildered public and shocked long-time observers of big business chicanery such as Sky News' Janine Perrett is the systematic exploitation of consumers who have a poor knowledge of financial products and legal consequences of decisions. Consider the fact that financial advisers and bankers have climbed on the shoulders of children, the infirm, the indigenous, the financially illiterate, the gambling addicted and stepped on the dead in order to reach for the bags of money that they would have viewed as being just reward for meeting the key performance indicators that were set by the organisations for which they worked.

Hold that thought while you also juggle the idea that people were either deployed in other parts of banks or had their employment terminated because they were unable to meet these targets. Add to that the fact that there were breaches of company law and anti-money laundering legislation that will be used as case studies by legal, accounting and corporate governance scholars in the future as examples of what never to do in a company that has the responsibility to look after people's funds with a degree of care.

This culture within the financial services space has been allowed to grow unchecked over time because the financial sector still maintained some degree of respectability in the eyes of the public that was reinforced with repeated assurances from the government – at one point under the leadership of Malcolm Turnbull – that there was no need for a royal commission and that a chat with bank chief executives from time to time during committee hearings would be sufficient to strike fear into the heart of the sector.

The biopsy that has been so publicly, incisively and forensically conducted by Hayne and his team has proven that this assertion was at best ill-founded.

Any wonder Perrett said she had never seen 'anything as appalling as what we are witnessing at the banking RC' in a tweet that was liked by thousands.

While the beauty parade of mea culpas from boards of directors and senior management of the banks are the start of a journey to rehabilitate tarnished reputations, do not forget that these systems were actually doing precisely what they were designed to do. Anyone suggesting that the model is broken needs to think twice about what model they are thinking about in their mind.

There is a maxim in the accounting world that plays out all over business: what gets measured, gets done. Measurement of performance in the many instances revealed during the stellar inquisitions by the incisive legal team led by Rowena Orr QC pointed to the detriments of a pure sales culture in an environment where the businesses concerned had a fiduciary duty to hold funds in trust.

Workers dedicated to ensuring they provide for their families will focus their minds on what is being measured in order to continue getting paid and to maintain employment. The banks designed a model that worked almost too well and internal controls – corporate monitoring procedures – failed to properly deal with breaches of internal procedure.

You give your money to a bank to hold on your behalf. That is all you might want them to do as a customer.

Spare a thought for every time your favourite teller you swapped stories about kids with was forced to ask you questions about switching from one kind of account to another in the hope you might make a decision that helped them stay put in a job that put bread and milk on the table. Problems also emerge when advisers craft advice to clients that are engineered to deliver a financial kick back from the sale of a product.

The question of whether commission-based remuneration is appropriate becomes relevant here.

It leads to one of the most important lessons to emerge from the Hayne Royal Commission and that is transactions involving a large slice of your savings or personal assets should not be undertaken without seeking a second opinion.

This must change.

We have now entered the era where a second opinion on significant financial transactions needs to be sought in the same way as you might seek a second opinion on a significant health issue because you need to know whether a course of action recommended is wise.

Might banks complain if customers seek external advice on their products? They might, but they've soiled their own nest.

APPENDIX 3

||||||||||||||||||||||||||||||||||||||||||||||

Hit them where it hurts

PUBLISHED ON 6 MAY 2018 IN THE COURIER MAIL

TIME TO GET TOUGH with corporate cowboys who can't walk a straight line.

Much has been said about the need to review penalties for directors and other company officers involved in bad corporate behaviour as a result of disturbing revelations about the conduct of financial institutions emerging from the Financial Services Royal Commission.

The discussion has also been propelled by the scathing report released in the past week by the Australian Prudential Regulation Authority into the calamity-ridden Commonwealth Bank.

There is great merit in revisiting and tweaking penalties for transgressions of company law periodically and the Turnbull Government's recently announced overhaul of penalties represents a good start but it is not enough.

The regulation of directors – especially directors of listed public companies that have been very naughty – needs a significant shake-up.

It is time that we treated directors, particularly those who are professional directors of public companies, as we do other professionals such as lawyers, doctors, tax agents, liquidators and auditors by establishing a statutory disciplinary board to deal with situations where directors as professionals have failed to comply with the law.

Some directors collect board positions the way kids collect football trading cards so regulating them as professionals makes sense.

The current law does provide for individuals to be banned from managing companies for up to five years if they meet certain conditions that include personal bankruptcy or the management of two or more companies that are trading while they are insolvent.

Existing laws must be extended, however, to incorporate a disciplinary regime so poor behaviour is penalised and better governance practice encouraged.

Mirroring the kind of disciplinary regimes that exist for auditors and tax agents would be a start.

Auditors and tax agents can get disciplined by separate statutory boards that have a range of penalties which include the removal of their statutory registration.

The range of penalties allows a disciplinary board to choose a penalty that is proportionate to the reported breach.

A new board to discipline directors, which would be made up of experienced directors as well as shareholder representatives, would need to be able to ban or 'red card' directors from holding an office of director for any public company for up to five years if breaches of law were proven.

A threat of a ban from serving on any public company board is one way of discouraging director complacency. Unblemished reputations mean the world to these folks.

There should also be a "yellow card" in the form of an undertaking to complete a course of education where it is clear a director failed to meet certain responsibilities because of a genuine lack of knowledge.

Public company directors who are lawyers are unlikely to fall into this category.

Any disciplinary action should be recorded on a public register so that community is aware the process delivers outcomes.

There is no reason why the community should tolerate poor behaviour from directors such as the conduct of the CBA board of directors highlighted in the APRA report.

A disciplinary process is required to keep professional directors on their toes.

ACKNOWLEDGEMENTS

A book like this can only be written with the assistance and encouragement of a range of people to whom I am eternally grateful. I thank Michael Wilkinson, the publisher, for taking this work on. Michael and I first worked together when he thought I could edit an accounting newsletter called Chartac Accountancy News back in the final quarter of 1995. I vividly remember the conversation over coffee with Michael near the escalator opposite a restaurant called Vivaldi's, which is no longer there and was replaced some years back by a chemist. That was a watershed moment for me and it has led to a productive, rewarding and challenging career. *Vulture City* brings me back to some of what I do best. Thanks also to Jess Lomas who has had to endure my quirks as an author in this process of getting the book together from cover art to proof edits and all of the other things that come with getting a book out the door.

Thank you to whistle blower Jeff Morris for both his courage in the face of corporate recalcitrance and his willingness to share his experiences so publicly with the community and in conversation with me during the writing of this book. The offices of several parliamentarians have been helpful in filling in the blanks when neither media coverage nor official records seemed to me to adequately tell the story. Special thanks to Peter Whish-Wilson who represents Tasmania in the Senate for the Greens for the time his team spent outlining their key concerns and their version of events to me. This was critical in being able to balance the public reportage and the evidence given before parliamentary committees. Thanks also to the work of journalistic colleagues such as Adele Ferguson from *The Age* and the *Sydney Morning Herald*. Various elements of the stories of banking conduct would not have been aired earlier had these stories not been told.

Colleagues in journalism have been both encouraging and helpful along this journey. My thanks to Peter Gleeson, the host of

Sky News' The Front Page, David Speers, Sky's political editor, Ross Greenwood, Channel Nine's finance guru and financial journalist, Janine Perrett, Sky News' presenter, Ian Rogers, founder and editor of Banking Day, and Quentin Dempster, the former host of the *7.30 Report*. Each of these individuals has taken some time out of their busy schedules to provide feedback and encouragement. Former Labor Senator Stephen Conroy has also been a valuable sounding board throughout the writing process. Colleagues and experts from within the accounting profession, including Professor Kevin Stevenson, Sir David Tweedie and Warren McGregor have provided valuable input and encouragement.

My immediate family has had to endure the tunnel vision that accompanies having an author in the family. I thank my parents, my brother Robert and sister-in-law Sally for their patience and understanding throughout the drafting process. They know what it has taken for me to achieve a range of things over my life.

Finally, I need to mention a person I and others in the accounting and business world saw as a mentor, the late Ken Spencer. Ken was a chairman and director of company boards, a partner in a major accounting firm and an individual that was known in Australia and overseas for his deep commitment to improving the transparency of reporting done by companies. Ken insisted at various times that I tackle corporate governance issues with as much gusto as I did the intricacies of the plumbing of corporate regulation. I eventually got there, Ken. Wish you were here.

'I found Tom to be someone who exemplified the best qualities of investigative journalism. He was persistent, knowledgeable, courageous and someone who researched his subject thoroughly. He was very much admired by the boards I chaired for his honesty, professionalism, trustworthiness and willingness to challenge. He was one of the finest journalists I met in my 20-plus years of setting accounting standards.'

SIR DAVID TWEEDIE, FORMER CHAIRMAN, INTERNATIONAL
ACCOUNTING STANDARDS BOARD

TOM RAVLIC is an investigative journalist, author and academic with more than 24 years' experience in reporting on and analysing politics and regulatory affairs for local and international media. He cut his teeth with almost a decade of journalism writing about accounting and finance and breaking stories for a range of print and online publications including metropolitan newspapers, business magazines, professional journals and overseas newsletters. Tom got his start with the industry newsletter Chartac Accountancy News and he has never taken a backward step.

Publications such as *The Age*, *CFO Magazine*, the newsletters from the Lafferty Publications stable on accounting, the Company Director and many others in print and online have benefitted from his depth of research and knowledge of a field often seen by some commentators as arcane. Tom is most proud of his investigative work that resulted in multiple cover stories in *CFO Magazine* while he was a contributor between January 1999 and December 2004. He returned to journalism in September 2016 after 12 years in professional associations in various roles dealing predominantly with regulatory analysis, government relations and risk management. His work has been published in *The Accountant, the International Accounting Bulletin, Retail Banker International, Crikey, PC and Tech Authority* and *The Saturday Paper* since his return to print.

His expertise in corporate governance, accounting and audit has been recognised with two casual academic appointments in recent years. Tom has lectured and tutored in auditing and assurance at both Deakin University and the University of Melbourne.

A collection of his writings was published in 2005 by John Wiley and Sons in a book called *Readings in Financial Reporting* for the academic market.

Tom has been a guest speaker at conferences, chaired panels comprised of regulatory figures from Australia and overseas and helped produce events designed to bring accountants and other professionals up to date with developments in corporate and financial regulation.

He is a Fellow of the Institute of Public Accountants and FINSIA and has several academic qualifications that include a Masters in Fraud and Financial Crime.